NATIONAL

CITIZEN
POWER

A CITIZEN LEADERSHIP MANUAL

INTRODUCING

The Art of
No-Blame Problem Solving

Harry S. Pozycki

A Cataloging-in-Publication record for this book
is available from the Library of Congress.

Library of Congress Cataloging-in Publication
Control Number 2020002099

978-1-9788-2073-9 paperback, 978-1-9788-2074-6 e-pub, 978-1-9788-2075-3 Mobi

CREDITS:
Interior images: Shutterstock.com, Getty Images, Dreamstime
Cover and book design by Olive M. Bryan

www.rutgersuniversitypress.org

Manufactured in the United States of America

TABLE OF CONTENTS

The *4* Power Centers:
Prime Decision-Making Arenas of Local Government
Introduction
- The Local Governing Body (Mayor & Council)
- The School Board
- The Planning Board/Commission
- The Local Political Party

Citizen Power in the 21ˢᵗ Century
- Expanded citizen problem solving power through advances in technology
- Expanded citizen rights to participate in government decision-making
  - Accessing current policy details (public records laws)
  - Introducing your solutions (public meetings acts/sunshine laws)

THE
CITIZENS
CAMPAIGN

■ DEDICATION PAGE ■

This book is dedicated to all citizens who want to learn how to become NO-BLAME Problem Solvers who can restore the values of service, civility, and pragmatism to America's political culture.

■ AUTHOR'S NOTE ■

Our elected representatives are overwhelmed with the volume of problems they are expected to resolve. For example, at the birth of our Nation, one member of the House of Representatives dealt with the problems of approximately 30,000 voters. Today they are trying to shoulder the problems of approximately 700,000 voters in their districts. Combine this with the fact that in the 21st century, technology and globalization have accelerated the formation and complexity of public problems, and you can begin to appreciate why our government representatives are having a hard time keeping pace. *Even worse, the resulting finger pointing is increasingly replacing problem solving and causing dangerous divisions in our society.*

To meet this challenge, we need to expand our Country's *problem solving* capacity. To do that, we need to envision a new role for citizens – one that goes beyond the ballot – one in which citizens can tap recent technological advances to turbocharge their search for proven solutions and exercise their new 21st century legal rights to participate in government problem solving decisions.

This book provides you with basic training in the use of these significant 21st century citizen powers, and importantly, it adds a step by step guide for No-Blame Problem Solving© that incorporates the strategies and tactics of highly successful practitioners of city and school district government.

Using these new legal and technological powers and this proven step-by-step problem solving process, we citizens can *lead our Country back onto the path of civility and pragmatism.* We don't have to sit on the sidelines while our government gridlocks and problems compound. We can become skilled problem solvers who know how to use the levers of government power to advance practical solutions. We can become "**citizen leaders**," and we can help our elected officials meet the challenges of this new century.

Even better, we can do this without leaving our hometowns. This book will introduce you to a variety of "non-elected," local, citizen leadership positions in which you can apply the powers of practical, No-Blame Problem Solving with both local and national impact. Terms of service in these positions range from one to three years, and the time commitment is quite manageable. This book will teach you how to access these positions and prepare you to participate in them.

One of the newest, and many say one of the most rewarding of these positions, is service as a Civic Trustee. This book will show you how to train for and apply to serve as a Civic Trustee in your own community.

Your participation and that of other citizen leaders will not only produce a pipeline of practical solutions, it will provide a powerful example of service, civility, and pragmatism that can heal today's political divide.

So I hope you choose to become a 21st century "citizen leader," to inspire your fellow citizens and rekindle the spirit of the great American barn raising, when we put our judgments of each other aside to get the barn built!

Harry S Pappas

■ ACKNOWLEDGEMENT ■

The Contents of this Manual are the result of twenty years of trial and error and lessons learned in the pursuit of state of the art citizen empowerment education. The input of dozens of Citizens Campaign staff, volunteer experts, and hundreds of citizens went into this work. Their observations of what worked and what didn't, were invaluable to the writing of this book and I would be remiss if I did not publicly acknowledge their contributions here.

I would also like to thank Rob Horowitz for his constant emphasis on "solutions that benefit the community as a whole" as the purpose of citizen empowerment. Power is useless unless it has purpose.

Last, but certainly not least, I want to thank Ellen Clarkson, Esq., Chief Operating Officer of The Citizens Campaign, for her research, writing and editing contributions. To say that this manual could not have been produced without her would be a gross understatement. Her deep appreciation of the "No-Blame" philosophy and the need to exercise it, not just in the governmental realm, but in all aspects of our lives, is inspiring to all of us.

■ INTRODUCTION ■

Our participatory roles as citizens have historically been limited to voting and protesting. But the 21st Century brings with it the powers needed to take on a new role. We can now become direct participants in government problem solving. In other words, we can become "players" in the game of government decision making.

So what's been holding us back? Remember when we were little kids, standing on the sidelines as the big kids played the game. We were afraid to get in the game because we didn't know the rules; we didn't know the positions; we didn't even know the basic plays.

This book will give you all you need to know to become successful players in the game of government problem solving and decision making. Read it, and you will never again be relegated to sitting on the sidelines, frustrated that you don't know how to get in the game.

THE PLAYING FIELDS

The first thing you need to know is where the playing fields of decision making are located that are accessible to you. It may surprise you to know that there are usually four playing fields in the game of political and governmental decision making located in your own back yard - your town or county.

Most of the major decision making in your community is made at: **1**) the governing body, often referred to as the Mayor and Council or, on the county level, the County Commissioners; **2**) the Planning Board; **3**) the School Board; and **4**) the local political parties. All four of these playing fields have one thing in common: they make final decisions that can improve your community.

Since they're located in your town or county, they are easily accesible playing fields where you have a right to get in the game of political and governmental decision making.

You can read about them in Chapter One.

THE RULES OF THE GAME

To get in the game, you also need to know the rules of the game. The rules in the political and governmental decision making arenas are your legal rights to participate directly in the decision making process. These rules were changed at the beginning of the 21st century to greatly increase citizens' ability to review the details of their towns' existing policies, and to introduce evidence based policies that woud improve their communities.

You will find the rules of the game in Chapter Two.

THE PLAYERS' EQUIPMENT

All games have equipment. The search engine is the most important piece of equipment in the game of government problem solving.

Chapter Two will show you how to use search engines to easily find successful, evidence based solutions that you can import for the betterment of your community, and which will make you a powerful player in the game of government decision making.

BASIC PLAYS OF THE GAME

As with any game, there are certain basic plays that give you a better chance of scoring, and in government decision making that means gaining adoption of the solutions you've found to improve your community. Chapters Three through Seven are packed with plays and strategies of successful practitioners of local government. These plays are contained in a No-Blame Problem Solving Guide regular citizens have used to pass hundreds of laws with a success rate of over 90%.

There are other plays that you may learn or even develop yourself, once you get some experience. But if you learn the basic plays explained in these chapters, you will be fully prepared to step onto the playing fields of government decision making.

THE PLAYERS' POSITIONS

Before you step on the playing field, you will want to decide what position is best for you. Four powerful positions are described in Chapter Eight. None of them require that you run for public office with the major time demands, fundraising requirements, and other challenges associated with doing this. The four roles or positions that you can choose from include:

1) appointed office holder on a local board or commission

2) local political party representative

3) solutions advocate in both social and conventional media and last but not least,

4) the position of Civic Trustee of your community

Each of these positions can give you the power of a player in the game of governmental decision making.

Chapter Eight will teach you about how you can access these positions and about the power that each provides.

— ▪ ▪ ▪ —

Once you've learned about the playing fields, the rules, the basic plays, and the citizen leadership positions in the game of government decision making, you won't need to run for public office to engage in meaningful public service and enjoy the honor that comes with it.

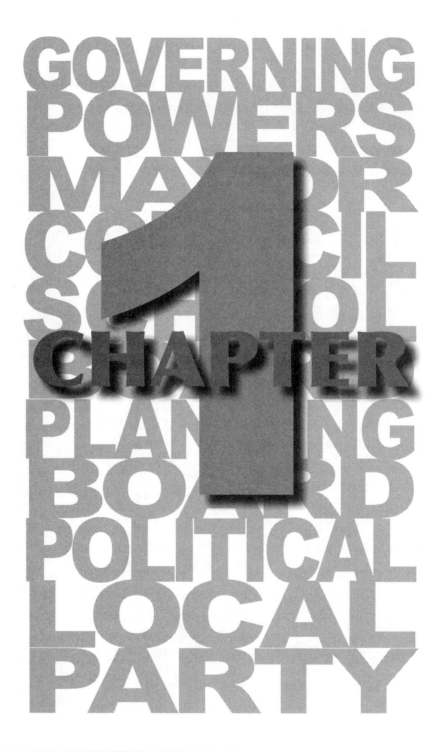

GOVERNING
POWERS
MAYOR
COUNCIL
SCHOOL
CHAPTER
PLANNING
BOARD
POLITICAL
LOCAL
PARTY

1

The 4 Power Centers

Prime Decision-Making Arenas of Local Government

The Local Governing Body (Mayor & Council)

The School Board

The Planning Board

The Local Political Party

INTRODUCTION

There are four major decision-making centers which are identified as "power centers" in this Manual. I refer to them as "power centers" because they are where power is exercised – where important decisions that will have major impacts on the community are made and, most importantly, where *final* decisions are made. The four main power centers are:

1 - **The local governing body or elected council & mayor**

2 - **The school board**

3 - **The planning board/commission**

4 - **The local political party**

Generally, the elected council, along with the mayor, determine what to include in the town budget and the amount of taxes paid by community residents. It also decides most overall policy questions.

Across the nation, there are some areas where these decisions are made at the County level. The school board, whether it is the local school board for your town or in some cases, a county school board, makes key educational decisions and is responsible for putting together the school budget.

The planning board or planning commission, through its power to devise and update the master plan, controls the physical development of the community. It is central to deciding what a community will look like, the quality of its environment and its plans for the future.

Lastly, the political party serves many powerful functions including choosing the candidates whom they endorse for public office, promoting citizens for influential appointed positions, and determining the issues to be prioritized in party platforms.

It is important to know that local government power centers have rules that set forth how items are put on their meeting agendas for decision-making. These also establish procedures for citizens to speak at their meetings, whether the citizen would like to merely ask a question on a matter to be voted on, or ask for time to make a presentation of a proposed solution.

Knowing these rules in advance when you are planning to go to a meeting and have a special purpose in mind, is always advisable.

And while such rules are increasingly available on government websites, if your city, town, county, or school board doesn't have it on their website, you can make a public records request for a copy.

GOVERNING BODY
(MAYOR AND COUNCIL)

The elected council serves as the legislative body of a municipality. It is usually where key tax, budget and policy decisions are made.

The council decides upon questions such as: should a municipality increase the number of police to cope with a rise in crime; should apartments be subject to rent control; should a tax abatement be agreed to.

MOST COMMUNITIES THROUGHOUT THE NATION HAVE MAYORS, BUT THEIR POWER AND LEGAL RELATIONSHIP TO THE COUNCIL VARY FROM COMMUNITY TO COMMUNITY.

Some mayors are elected separately by a community wide vote; some are chosen by the council from among its members. Many mayors function similarly to governors and presidents as the chief executive officer of a community. In many communities throughout the nation, elected officials delegate much of their authority to an appointed town manager or administrator. If this is true in your community, this is definitely a person you want to get to know.

City and town councils also vary in how their members are elected: some by a community-wide vote, i.e., members are elected at large, and others, where the community is divided into council wards, residents of each ward elect their own council member as well as electing members at large.

IN ANY CASE, COUNCILS, WHATEVER THEIR COMPOSITION, DECIDE MOST MATTERS THAT COME BEFORE THEM BY A MAJORITY VOTE.

In most communities, however, the mayor has the right to veto a measure passed by the council, and it usually takes a two-thirds vote of the full council membership to override a veto.

IN ORDER TO PARTICIPATE MOST EFFECTIVELY IN YOUR LOCAL GOVERNMENT, IT IS IMPORTANT TO KNOW HOW IT IS ORGANIZED.

The best ways to obtain this information are to call or write to the municipal clerk and ask them the following questions, and/or do some research and find this information out on your own by visiting the town/ county's official website:

- **How is the mayor elected?**
- **How many council members are there?**
- **Are the council members elected community-wide, by ward or by some combination of the two?**
- **What power does the mayor have to veto council votes?**
- **How many council votes does it take to override a veto?**
- **Is there an appointed Town Manager who runs the day-to-day operations of government?**

Most Councils are required to hold a public hearing on ordinances (local laws) before a final vote on their adoption. This usually presents an opportunity for citizens to comment on and to ask questions about the proposed ordinances.

However, in certain states, like New Jersey for example, this opportunity is only present at "**regular**" meetings of the Council, as opposed to "**agenda**" meetings where proposed ordinances can be "introduced" but not voted into law.

While in most states there is no specific requirement to set aside a portion of Council meetings for public input, most communities do provide a public comment period at Council meetings. This provides an opportunity for citizens to raise and speak about their own issues and proposals.

HOWEVER, IT IS IMPORTANT TO NOTE THAT COUNCILS USUALLY ADOPT RULES SETTING UP PROCEDURES FOR PUBLIC INPUT.

Such rules may include the length of time a citizen has to make remarks, when they can speak at the meeting, and whether the comments must be limited to the items on the meeting agenda. There can even be a requirement that citizens sign up either in advance of the meeting or at the beginning of the meeting if they wish to speak at all.

It is again worth noting that local government power centers have rules that set forth how items are put on their meeting agendas for discussion or decision-making, as well as the procedures for conducting their meetings.

These are called "**administrative codes**." Knowing these rules and procedures in advance when you are planning to present a proposed solution is always advisable. And while such rules are increasingly available on government websites, if your city/county doesn't have it on their website, you can make a public records request for a copy.

THE SCHOOL BOARD

The local school board oversees public education in a community from pre-kindergarten through high school. It sets overall policies which ensure quality teaching, sound fiscal management and adequate facilities.

**Thus, your local school board
decides many important questions including:**

- how much teachers will be paid;
- what professional development efforts to improve teacher performance will be funded;
- and when to propose new school construction or renovations.

Importantly, the school board hires the superintendent of schools who is responsible for implementing policies set by the board. (It should be noted however, that in some cities, the Superintendent is selected by the Mayor).

FURTHER, while there are general statewide curriculum guidelines and required standardized tests, local school boards still maintain a broad amount of discretion with regard to decision-making around curriculum.

In a few cases, where school districts have consistently performed poorly and there are questions of mismanagement, state law allows the state to take over the management of the school district.

In these instances, the state appoints a school superintendent and the local board of education's role is reduced to a largely advisory function.

In a small number of communities, usually large cities, the mayor appoints the members of the school board. However, the vast majority of American communities have elected school boards.

IF YOU ARE INTERESTED IN EDUCATION ISSUES, YOU SHOULD FIND OUT IF YOUR SCHOOL BOARD IS ELECTED OR APPOINTED AS THIS MAY DETERMINE WHAT STRATEGIES YOU EMPLOY TO HAVE AN IMPACT ON ANY DECISIONS MADE BY THE BOARD.

You can usually find this out with a simple direct call to the school board. If a school board is elected, it will be critical to make your case directly to them.

If appointed, it will also be important to make your concerns known to the mayor as he/she is likely to have a fair amount of influence over the members he/she has appointed. In those instances where a state has taken over the operation of a school district, citizens should concentrate their efforts on influencing their state legislators, the state education commissioner, the governor's office as well as the local school board.

If you are interested in addressing education issues as a problem solver, you should become familiar with the workings of your Board of Education and your rights as a citizen to impact its decisions.

Toward this end, you should obtain a copy of the Board's policies and procedures and review the sections on board governance.

While most states do not have a specific requirement mandating a public comment period during school board meetings, most communities often provide one. The board usually sets rules governing when and how long a person may speak at a meeting.

THE PLANNING BOARD

The planning board or planning commission makes key environmental and growth decisions and as a result, is central in determining the physical development of a community and its resulting quality of life.

The composition of planning boards vary from state to state, but are usually comprised of a combination of elected officials, citizen members and government officials who are appointed by the local governing body (and/or the mayor).

The planning board is responsible for the development of a master plan for the community and for a review and update of the plan. However, in most communities, be aware that the master plan can be amended at any time. *The master plan provides a road map for how a community will grow.*

It addresses questions such as what part of the community will be reserved for residences and at what density levels, and in what areas commercial development will be permitted. *A housing plan element is sometimes a component of the master plan and in some states includes a provision for affordable housing.*

In some states, the planning board also has the legal right to include several other elements in the master plan such as:

- a sub-plan for conservation of the town's environment and open spaces
- an economic plan
- circulation plan
- recycling plan
- and capital improvement plan

All of which help define and direct a town's future development and growth. Importantly, zoning regulations must be consistent with the master plan.

Thus, the master plan is a document with teeth, and citizens can play an important role in determining its contents and impacting their community's future.

The planning board usually has the responsibility to review and hold public hearings on proposals for new development, but it's often too late to raise concerns when the planning board is hearing a proposal for development, especially when the proposal meets all the standards set forth in the zoning regulations.

Citizens have the most power to affect development when they make input on the town's master plan amendment, and as noted above, in some communities, the planning board may amend its master plan at any time.

Given that the composition of the planning board is elected officials and people appointed by elected officials, it is not surprising that the municipal master plan is often subject to political influence.

CITIZEN ACTION AND ACTIVITY CAN ABSOLUTELY HAVE A MAJOR IMPACT ON PLANNING BOARD DECISIONS AND CAN OFTEN BE A COUNTERWEIGHT TO LOBBYING BY DEVELOPERS AND OTHER INTERESTED PARTIES.

THE LOCAL POLITICAL PARTY

The local political parties represent a power center of which many citizens are not aware. Of those who are aware, most lack the knowledge about how an ordinary citizen can access power and advance proposed solutions through them.

This is noteworthy when you consider that local party representatives, usually elected at the neighborhood level, not only have the ability to award party endorsements of candidates for town or city or county office, they also have power over candidate endorsements far beyond the local level.

FURTHERMORE, LOCAL PARTY REPRESENTATIVES OFTEN HAVE STRONG INFLUENCE IN THE SELECTION OF CITIZENS TO SERVE IN HUNDREDS OF GOVERNMENT POSITIONS, BOTH PAID AND UNPAID.

The lack of citizen awareness of local political parties and how they work is regrettable given that the office of neighborhood party representative, (also referred to as a party "**committee member**,") which exists in most communities and/or counties *– is the closest and most accessible elected position for entry into public life.*

The posts of party committee member are filled by *four citizens* per election district who are elected during the the primary election to represent a single neighborhood of roughly 700 to 1,000 voters.

It is important to understand that this political system provides these neighborhood committee positions in order to exercise its power at the grassroots level.

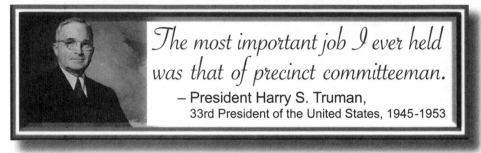

The most important job I ever held was that of precinct committeeman.
– President Harry S. Truman,
33rd President of the United States, 1945-1953

Even if one is not interested in or able to run for a party committee seat, it is important to know about the roles and powers of these neighborhood party representatives since they have influence over the elected and appointed officials of their respective parties.

In many cases, party committee members also have influence with officials elected in non-partisan elections, where party labels are not listed on the ballot but party endorsements and the money and organizing power that come with it remains a major factor.

This is also the case because party committee members are often looked to by voters in their neighborhoods for information and advice about candidates for all offices.

Additionally, most officials, even if elected in non-partisan elections, do have a party membership and may aspire to fill party posts or future public office on the party ticket. They know that party committee members are important to their dreams of advancement.

Thus, whether a public official is elected in a partisan or non-partisan election, if a citizen needs to get their attention, one of the most effective routes is through the party committee member.

To find out more information about the specifics of the political party structure in your state and local area, visit the following websites:

 Association of State Democratic Committees at: https://asdc.democrats.org/state-parties/

Republican Party State Leadership at: https://gop.com/leaders/states/

EXPANDED PROBLEM SOLVING TECHNOLOGY PUBLIC RECORDS OPRA/PRA PRACTICAL SOLUTIONS

CHAPTER

2

Citizen Power in the 21st Century

- Expanded citizen problem solving power through advances in technology
- Expanded citizen rights to participate in government decision-making
- Accessing current policy details (public records laws)
- Introducing your solutions (public meeting acts/sunshine laws)

The 21st century has ushered in new citizen powers and new ways to exercise them. This can have a tremendous impact on our historically passive and reactive roles. We don't have to wait on the sidelines for our government officials to act. We are no longer limited to protesting or "voting the bums out."

We now have the power to become proactive citizen leaders solving problems and advancing practical solutions to today's challenges without waiting for the political establishment to act.

USE TECHNOLOGICAL TOOLS AND RESOURCES TO EXPAND YOUR CITIZEN POWER

The phrase "knowledge is power" may be a cliché, but it is more true than ever in today's civic arena. If we want to play a role as practical problem solvers, working to find and offer solutions to the real and pressing issues facing our communities, we have to be able to research, compare and share solutions that have been successful in cities and towns across the nation and even around the world.

In the past, time-consuming comparative analysis of government policies in other cities or school districts was largely the province of *full time* government staff, like city administrators, and often required some expertise.

But now, using the internet, and search engines like Google and Bing, this type of research can be done by regular citizens with limited time. Citizens can research workable solutions that have produced cost effective positive effects in other cities and offer them for adoption in their own hometowns.

YOU HAVE EXPANDED CITIZEN POWER THROUGH MODERN ADVANCES IN TECHNOLOGY

The meteoric rise of the internet in our time has had a profound effect on our ability to engage and take an active role in the governing of our communities and country.

Now, citizens can play a significant role in improving government problem solving by searching for successful policies at work in similar communities and offering them for consideration in their own towns.

CITIZENS CAN EXPAND GOVERNMENT PROBLEM SOLVING CAPACITY AND SHIFT THE POLITICAL FOCUS FROM WHO HAS THE POWER TO WHO HAS THE SOLUTION.

Now, citizen problem solvers can commit to better their communities by researching and advancing practical solutions to community issues and challenges. Practical solutions are based on evidence of success- which means they have been demonstrated to work in communities similar to our own.

"Searching" on the internet via Google or any search engine allows us to find, analyze and compare policies that are working well in other communities, while also researching news articles, expert opinions, studies, public documents, and more. At the same time, we can rely on technology via social media channels and apps to "share" our findings with fellow problem solvers, with government officials, and with the greater community.

All 50 states have public records acts (**PRA**), variously known as sunshine laws, public records acts, freedom of information laws, etc. *While these laws vary in strength, generally speaking, they are one of the most powerful tools in the citizens' arsenal.*

(A detailed description of every state's public records laws can be found at **https://www.rcfp.org/open-government-guide** and an abbreviated, more general outline can be found at **https://www.nfoic.org/coalitions/state-foi-resources/state-freedom-ofinformation-laws**)

PRAs ensure your right to access and examine the details of government policies made by a government or public agency in the course of public business, including your local government and board of education. Records including paper documents, electronic files, audio recordings, etc., reveal such policy details as costs, the staff responsible for policy implementation, time limits for action, and more.

Historically, most records were legally considered government property, accessible only to government officials, and this did not include ordinary citizens like you and me. Passage of PRAs reversed that thinking, and now such records are considered the property of the people.

This puts all of us, citizens and the government officials who represent us, on a level playing field in terms of access to information.

Following are the basics and practical How-to's for exercising our new civic powers under PRAs

HOW-TO USE YOUR STATE'S PUBLIC RECORDS LAW - **PRA**

So once you've made the decision to become a problem solver and have determined the issue you are passionate about, you can investigate what your city or town has done in the past, and is currently doing.

You can begin your research by simply exploring your city's website for information; or reading news items and checking for any media coverage on the issue; or calling and speaking with the city clerk or other government office which may have information.

But the most powerful way to get this information is through the exercise of your rights under your state's public records law (**PRA**).

Filing a public records (**PRA**) request gives you the most effective and thorough way to find out if and how your city, town, or county government and/or school board may be dealing with your chosen issue. This gives you the ability to compare your local government entity's existing policy to those solutions you find to be successful in cities and towns similar to your own.

GET A STANDARD PUBLIC RECORDS (PRA) REQUEST FORM OR DRAFT YOUR OWN

Anyone can file a public records request (PRA) form.
Sample request letters for your state can be downloaded at:

https://www.nfoic.org/organizations/state-sample-foia-request-letters

(Please note: Request forms or instructions regarding the information you need to include if you are drafting your own request are often available on the city, town or county government and/or school board website.)

DRAFTING THE PRA REQUEST LETTER AND/OR COMPLETING THE REQUEST FORM

This is an important step for several reasons. Generally speaking, state public records laws do not give you the right to simply ask for information. You need to ask for a specific

document. If your request is not specific enough, you might get voluminous copies of documents that you may have to sift through to get the information you really need. Ask for documents that reveal the policy you are researching. You don't want to have to file several requests that would extend the time for you to get all the information you need.

SO REMEMBER, A PUBLIC RECORDS (PRA) REQUEST IS FOR WRITTEN RECORDS OR DOCUMENTATION, NOT GENERAL INFORMATION

Here is a list of possible documents that may be requested if you are researching municipal policies:

- Ordinances
- Executive Orders;
- Resolutions – identify public body; possible date parameters
- Government memoranda;
- Government contracts – identify possible parties;
- Audits;
- Minutes of meetings – if possible, narrow down on meeting dates
- Closed session meeting minutes;
- Budgets (including staff salaries);
- Reports;
- Emails – identify sender or recipient; a reasonable date range; a reasonable subject matter

SUBMITTING THE PUBLIC RECORDS (PRA) REQUEST FORM

You can submit the public records (PRA) request letter or form by delivering it in person during regular business hours, or by mail, fax or electronically to the appropriate custodian of records.

Confirm with the local government entity you are requesting the record from: **1-** the person who should receive it, and **2-** the preferred method of transmission.

In most states, you also have the right to view and inspect records in person in the office where they are kept.

OFFICIAL RESPONSE TO A PUBLIC RECORDS (PRA) REQUEST & WHAT YOU CAN DO

A municipality/public agency must respond to a PRA request within the time frame specified in your state's law unless it is particularly lengthy or otherwise difficult to fulfill.

Generally speaking, the response must be in writing. The request can either be granted; denied; require more clarity or an extension of time to respond.

Sometimes the person responsible for providing the records to you will call you if clarification is needed; *and it is advisable to follow up if the specified amount of time has gone by and you haven't heard anything.*

SUCH COMMUNICATION CAN AFFORD YOU AN OPPORTUNITY TO BUILD A POSITIVE RELATIONSHIP WITH YOUR LOCAL OFFICIALS AND THE LOCAL GOVERNMENT EMPLOYEES WHO SERVE YOUR COMMUNITY.

They usually know a lot and can provide useful information on a less formal basis. They can also become a resource for you as you proceed to develop your solutions and down the road present them to public officials.

 However, if the response is a denial of your request, look at the list of records that have been specifically excluded from public access under your state's public records statute and determine if your request legitimately falls within one of the exceptions.

There are a limited number of sensitive items, like personnel matters, ongoing litigation materials, and current contract negotiations, which are ordinarily not available under public records laws; however, these exceptions vary state by state.

Some state laws enable a government entity to also deny your request if it concludes that such a request would substantially disrupt agency operations and a reasonable solution can't be worked out between you. But the burden usually remains on a municipality or county government to demonstrate a compelling interest in keeping documents secret and out of the public eye.

So, if you don't agree with government officials that the information you are seeking is legitimately private, you can try to negotiate with officials and/or revise your request so you might get the information you are seeking in another way, or you can file an **APPEAL**.

For the specific way to appeal in your state, visit **https://www.rcfp.org/open-government-guide.**

COSTS: INSPECTING RECORDS IS FREE; COPYING/ REPRODUCING RECORDS IS NOT; SOME SPECIAL FEES MAY ALSO APPLY IN CERTAIN SITUATIONS

You can usually go to a public agency office during normal business hours and request to look at public records. There is no charge for doing this, however, if you want copies of records, there is almost always a charge. To find out the amount, check with the local government entity you are requesting the records from, or examine your state law and see if the fees are set forth.

Another option to explore, is requesting to have records emailed. In most states, the agency is required to inform you about any costs that may be involved, and it may
also require a deposit if the costs are above a certain amount.

Some states provide guides to their public records laws. For example, **A Citizens Guide to OPRA**, published by The State of New Jersey, is available on the state's website at

www.nj.gov/opra

The guide provides information and answers to frequently asked questions about New Jersey's OPRA law.

 OPRA is a New Jersey statute that governs the public's access to government records in New Jersey. The law is compiled in the statutes as N.J.S.A. 47:1A-1 et seq.

Specifically, OPRA is intended to:
- Expand the public's right of access to government records;
- Create an administrative appeals process if access is denied;
- Define what records are and are not "government records."

YOU HAVE A "RIGHT TO SPEAK" AT MEETINGS OF LOCAL GOVERNING BODIES UNDER STATE OPEN PUBLIC MEETINGS ACTS (OPMA), AND MOST CITIES, TOWNS AND COUNTIES PROVIDE PUBLIC COMMENT PERIODS AT THESE MEETINGS

State Open Public Meeting Acts in all 50 states provide a right to attend local council meetings, along with most other government meetings. Several states take the next step and provide a right to comment.

In a few states, such as New Jersey, a right to present your own solution for adoption is explicitly provided. Be sure to take a look at your state's OPMA at:

https://www.rcfp.org/open-government-guide

Fueled in large measure by states adopting open public meeting acts which created an expectation of public participation, most local government entities throughout the nation do provide a comment period at their meetings and permit residents to present their own proposals. Time restrictions and other rules governing citizen participation in local government meetings are usually available on city, town and county government websites.

OPEN PUBLIC MEETINGS ACTS (OPMA)

Similar to PRAs, the Open Public Meetings Acts or OPMAs, sometimes known as Sunshine Laws, were adopted to ensure transparency in our government decision-making processes.

Citizens should be able to *"witness in full detail all phases of the deliberation, policy formulation and decision making of public bodies."* (New Jersey's OPMA)

This purpose was considered by state legislatures to be *"vital to the enhancement and proper functioning of the democratic process"* as secrecy in public affairs undermines both the government's role as well as that of citizens.

While OPMA laws vary from state to state, they by and large apply to public bodies, which are voting bodies that are empowered to spend public funds or that affect persons' rights.

Thus the city, town or county council, school board and planning board/commission usually all fall under its purview. Generally speaking, OPMAs require covered government bodies to:

■ Afford adequate advance public notice of their meetings.

■ Ensure that all citizens have the right to attend and videotape those meetings.

■ Formally let the public know when the body is going into closed session and will be excluding the public and the reasons for doing so.

■ Keep minutes of all meetings which should be promptly made available to the public, as well as minutes of closed sessions, which should be made available at an appropriate time, meaning when the reason for keeping the matter closed no longer exists.

Most local government entities in our nation set aside a time for public input at city council and school board meetings. This is especially relevant to our role as problem solvers.

This right allows regular citizens to present their solutions to government officials and the public, and thereby become partners with their elected officials in expanding their communities' *problem solving* capacity.
(In Chapter 5, we will discuss the do's and don'ts for making an effective presentation.)

It must be noted, however, that when a public body sets aside time for public comment, it nearly always provides rules for the comment period.

 **FOR EXAMPLE,** there can be a *time limit* placed on speakers; also there may be a requirement that speakers *register* to indicate their intention to speak in advance of the meeting or simply at the beginning of the meeting.

PUTTING OPMA AND ITS PRINCIPLES TO WORK FOR YOU

There are various ways that your rights under your state's OPMA laws to attend government meetings, and in many states, to also provide an opportunity to make public comment at such meetings, that can help you play a role in our government's decision-making process.

FOR EXAMPLE, you can introduce proposed school curriculum changes and additions at a school board meeting; or you may attend a planning board hearing to offer proposed revisions to your city's or county's master plan.

You can also attend any and all council meetings to propose practical, evidence-based solutions which have been successful in similar cities or towns.

HERE ARE SOME GENERAL POINTERS WHEN YOU ATTEND PUBLIC GOVERNMENT MEETINGS:

 Get General Information about the meeting times, dates and locations of the meetings you are interested in attending

Know the Rules for Citizen Input – when during the meeting can citizens speak? Do citizens have to indicate in advance that they want to speak at the meeting? Are there time limits for speaking?

Request Permission in advance to be placed on the agenda and present your own proposal if your city council or other local governing body only permits comment on current agenda items. Our experience is that such a request is often honored.

Be Respectful at all times, even when challenged or others are rude or dismissive to you – you will get better and more positive results if you are respectful of all participants whether you are asking a question or making a statement

Arrive Early – this will give you an opportunity to meet and maybe chat with government officials before the meeting starts – you can pick up and review a copy of the meeting agenda so you know how meeting matters are prioritized – you can speak with the clerk or secretary to ask if there's a sign-up sheet or any other information that may be helpful for the public to know – you can introduce yourself to public officials and to any media people covering the meeting – you can meet your neighbors and other citizens who may also be interested in a specific issue.

3PRINCIPLES
POWER
PRACTICAL
SOLUTIONS
EVIDENCE
PRAGMATIC
CHAPTER
3
COST
EFFECTIVE
BENEFICIAL
COMMUNITY

CHAPTER THREE

The Power of Practical Solutions:
The *3* Principles of Pragmatic Problem Solving

1 Solutions should be based on
  evidence of success

2 Solutions should be cost effective

3 Solutions should be beneficial to
  the community as a whole

**To identify a problem is to complain
– usually with no positive result.
To identify a problem *AND* offer a solution is
to lead, and to better your community.**

Citizens often appear before their city council or school board when a problem arises, for example, a problem with flooding or a problem with student discipline. They feel that by bringing the problem to the officials' attention, they have done their duty; and they are right, but only in part.

They would be much more effective if they offered a solution, or even just a first step towards a solution, that could improve the situation and benefit their community.

Local public officials often shoulder an extensive list of ongoing responsibilities and face multiple issues in representing the communities they serve. ***They can use your help!***

You can learn how to find and present practical solutions that have been proven to work, for adoption by your local government or school board. You can become a problem solver and get results on ***the issues you care about!***

The democratic principles and values inherent in the role of citizen problem solver have roots going back to the ancient Greek city-state of Athens, the birthplace of modern democracy.

Upon reaching maturity, young Athenians stood together in the public square and took an oath to uphold the public's civic duty – to leave their city not less, but greater and more beautiful than it was left to them.

In the same way, when we take action in the role of problem solver, we are acting on a pledge *"to leave our community and country better than we found them by pursuing solutions instead of just pointing out problems and assigning blame."*

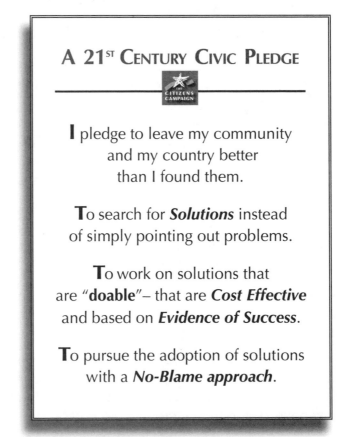

A 21ˢᵀ CENTURY CIVIC PLEDGE

I pledge to leave my community
and my country better
than I found them.

To search for **Solutions** instead
of simply pointing out problems.

To work on solutions that
are **"doable"**– that are **Cost Effective**
and based on **Evidence of Success**.

To pursue the adoption of solutions
with a **No-Blame approach**.

TO BE A TRULY EFFECTIVE PROBLEM SOLVER, YOUR SOLUTIONS SHOULD BE IN KEEPING WITH THESE **3** PRINCIPLES:

THEY SHOULD BE BASED ON EVIDENCE OF SUCCESS.
Simply put, this means the solution has been demonstrated to work in towns and cities similar to your own.

THEY SHOULD BE COST EFFECTIVE.
Basically, this means that the solution you are proposing is cost-saving or neutral in its impact on your town or city's budget.

THEY SHOULD BE BENEFICIAL TO THE COMMUNITY AS A WHOLE.
This means that the solution you are proposing will be of benefit to the greater community, not just your block, your home, or your personal interest.

Practical solutions embody these distinguishing characteristics because when they are based on evidence of success, they are less vulnerable to ideological opposition; when they are cost effective, they are not constrained by tight budgets; when they benefit the community as a whole, self-interest does not become an issue.

Thousands of citizens have been successful at finding, developing and advancing practical solutions in their cities and towns. These include policies that have improved police/community relations; policies that have saved millions of taxpayer dollars in government contracting; and policies that have helped make our communities more prepared to handle severe weather conditions.

In the chapters that follow you will learn how to find, develop and advance "practical" solutions so that you will have the best chance of success in getting your proposed solutions adopted.

CHAPTER 4

COURTESY BENEFITS DO THE NO BLAME

The Power of the No-Blame Approach

The "**No-Blame**" strategy for advancing solutions in the arena of politics and government is a lot more than a matter of courtesy. It is a powerful and sophisticated political strategy which keeps the focus on your solution and increases your ability to make progress.

A "NO-BLAME" APPROACH HAS SEVERAL BENEFITS

FIRST – and perhaps most importantly, it keeps you from being marginalized. When you approach an issue by blaming officials for a bad policy or for their failure to solve a problem, you can easily be cast as a gadfly or crank, and you lose credibility.

SECOND – a "No-Blame" approach keeps officials from becoming defensive and turning off to the benefits of your solution. The smart move is to find something in the current policy that you can agree with and offer to help make it better. Becoming "**the helper**" puts you on the side of the officials you are trying to convince.

ANOTHER WAY TO KEEP OFFICIALS FROM BECOMING DEFENSIVE AND WORKING TO SHUT DOWN YOUR PROPOSAL, IS TO RECOGNIZE THEIR GOOD INTENTIONS.

Working as a "helper" to achieve the good intentions of elected officials also permits you to be open minded to their concerns and to shape your solution to deal with any of the official's objections while still keeping the core tenets of your proposal intact. We call this *"doing the doable."*

FINALLY, remember that you will need support from the media and the public as you pursue adoption of your solution.

IN THIS CASE THE OLD AXIOM THAT, "IF YOU GIVE RESPECT, YOU COMMAND RESPECT" APPLIES.

In other words, you can keep the pressure on for adoption of your solution if you keep the respect of the press and the voters.

It's good to remember that as a citizen problem solver, your purpose is to **serve together** with your elected officials in the pursuance of practical solutions.

IT IS NOT YOUR IDEA VERSUS THEIR IDEA

A remarkable example of the power of the No-Blame approach can be found in Dr. Martin Luther King's success. Dr. King overcame immense opposition to the Voting Rights Act of 1965 by using a strategy of non-violence, in other words, a no-blame approach that kept the focus on his solution until its adoption was unavoidable.

Reverend Martin Luther King, Jr. with President Lyndon B. Johnson at the signing of the Voting Rights Act of 1965.

STRATEGY
IDENTIFY

CHAPTER

5

IMPLEMENTION
RESPECTFUL
PURSUIT
ADOPTION

CHAPTER FIVE

Using the Strategy of No-Blame Problem Solving

- Identifying Your Issue and Finding Solutions
- Adapting Your Solution to Make It "Doable"
- Presenting Your Solution for Adoption
- Respectful Pursuit to Implementation of Your Solution

IDENTIFYING YOUR ISSUE AND FINDING SOLUTIONS

We know that today's technology has often been used to communicate a global dimension to many problems, and that it has also expanded our awareness of pervasive and significant underlying problems like racial injustice. But we already know that many of the problems we face in the 21st century are complex and substantial.

So, the first step to be taken regarding the issue you care about, is to discuss and identify the broad policy areas that you (and your group) are passionate about. For example, are you interested in problems in the environmental arena, or in the area of education, or in public safety? Some of the broad areas that most citizens are generally interested in are:

- Education
- Public Safety
- Environment
- Government Innovation/Reform & Waste-Cutting
- Economic Development

Next, moving from these broad categories, "**drill down**" to a more specific problem that you believe you can tackle with a "doable" solution. Some examples of more specific problems are:

- safety in your city's parks;
- abandoned and deteriorating properties affecting your neighborhood;   or
- discipline policies in your child's schools.

Now you may have identified several problems, so it's time to prioritize. Consider the following in doing so:

- ❏ if working in a group, which issues are of most concern?
- ❏ what community assistance can be expected in support of this issue?
- ❏ how politically difficult is the problem?
- ❏ how big is the scope of the problem?
- ❏ how opportune is the time to address the problem?

SUBMIT A PRA REQUEST

So, once you've made the decision to become a problem solver and have determined the specific issue you are passionate about, you need to investigate what your city, town or county has done thus far to address the issue.

In other words, what is the current policy?

You can begin your research by simply exploring your local government entity's website for information; – or reading news items and checking for any media coverage on the issue; – or calling and speaking with local government officials who may have information.

But the most powerful way to get this information is through the exercise of your rights under your state's public records act (PRA).

Filing a public records/PRA request gives you the most effective and thorough way to find out if and how your local government entity is dealing with your chosen issue.

This gives you the ability to compare your local government entity's existing policy to those solutions you may find to be successful in cities, towns or counties similar to your own.

MOVING BEYOND **PRA** REQUESTS - CONDUCTING BROADER EVIDENCE-BASED RESEARCH

Filing a public records (PRA) request to determine how your city/town/county is dealing with an issue represents the beginning of your search for a solution.

It will not only inform you about the current policy, it will suggest words that you can "search" and other details that will help you conduct broader evidence-based research, as you look at how other communities similar to your own have addressed the problem.

This can be accomplished by pursuing several avenues

■ An internet search utilizing appropriate key words is the place to start. **FOR EXAMPLE**, if your chosen issue is in the  area of "education," narrowed down to "bullying and student behavior" in schools, you could use the key words "best practices, student discipline policies" to begin your search. If the first 10 items that come up on your search don't appear relevant, try narrowing your search with other key words.

■ Next, check websites of colleges and universities and connect with specific departments or academic centers that deal with your chosen issue.

■ Do the same for professional associations and organizations with a focus on local government or specialty subjects. Here are a few selected examples from around the nation:

Michigan Municipal League, Colorado Association of School Boards, Georgia Economic Developers Association, Association of New Jersey Environmental Commissions.

Your state should have similar organizations.

■ In all of these research strategies, look for policy papers, news stories, articles in newspapers and respected publications, expert opinion columns, and the like, for information about the issue and  solutions that have been implemented with successful results.

■ When evaluating your results, make sure the solutions you found have been implemented in cities, towns and/or counties similar to your own – **FOR EXAMPLE**, in terms of the size of the city or school board budget, size of population, economics, demographics, etc.

■ Also, utilize media literacy skills when conducting your research to confirm the authenticity and value of the sources of information.

(See Chapter 7 on Media Literacy in the Search for Solutions)

ADAPTING YOUR SOLUTION TO MAKE IT "DOABLE"

Now you're at a point where you've determined the current policy through your public records (PRA) requests and conducted your own evidence based research for best practice solutions.

t's time to sift through the information you've gathered and then shape it with information relating to the practicality of implementing the solution you are proposing.

✔ Using the information gathered via public records and your evidence-based research for successful solutions, determine which type of solution may be the best fit taking into consideration where your community's current policy is and where you want it to be.

✔ Review the details of the current policy you received through the public records you've obtained and determine what measures may be in place and what actions your city/town/county has taken with regard to the issue.

✔ Follow-up with the appropriate parties, for example, the city clerk, the official responsible for running a program, the budget officer, etc

✔ Also, connect with members of your community, professors and individuals at local academic institutions and associations who may have significant knowledge about policy implementation, program costs, challenges, evidence of success, etc.

✔ Most importantly, find out what, if any, new staff were required in implementing the solution you identified and how long it took to successfully implement.

✔ Then, analyze all the information you collected, and tailor your solution to build upon the positive aspects of the current policy and take into consideration any ongoing efforts by officials to improve it.

✔ Finally, consider the available staff and funding before you decide how big a change in policy you propose as the first step toward your ultimate goal.

MAKE SURE IT'S COST EFFECTIVE

One of the most important aspects of any proposed solution concerns cost. How much will it cost to implement the solution and where would the money come from? Answers to these questions are especially relevant in today's fiscally-challenged and economically disadvantaged cities.

■ Determine what costs will be associated with implementing your proposed solution.

■ Evaluate possible costs such as administrative costs, staff time and new hires, as well as any potential savings.

■ Look at your city, town or county's budget with an eye on possible line items that might cover any new or additional costs.

■ By the same token, look at the budget to determine whether there may be areas from which savings could be generated to offset possible new costs.

■ If it turns out that implementing the solution is not covered or only partially covered by the municipal or county budget, explore and suggest alternative funding sources such as grants, crowd-funding, and special campaigns.

■ Alternatively, you might determine that the solution is cost-neutral, with little or no impact, or better yet, that the solution results in cost savings, whether immediately or in the long-run.

UNDERSTANDING AND BEING ABLE TO EXPLAIN THE COSTS OF IMPLEMENTATION OF A SOLUTION IS A PREREQUISITE TO ANY PRESENTATION OR SOLICITATION FOR SUPPORT FOR ITS ADOPTION.

DO THE DOABLE

Getting anything done in the politically contentious world is a challenge. Moreover, in trying to find solutions addressing the problems in our communities, it is helpful to understand that most issues in today's world are often complex and without simple or cost-effective solutions.

Therefore, when you are seeking to address a problem that may be considered pervasive or multi-faceted, or perhaps costly to take on, it is advisable to learn to **"do the doable,"** that means breaking your solution down into parts or steps.

FOR EXAMPLE:

■ Offering to **"phase in"** a solution, accommodates implementing the solution over time, (i.e., phases), and may allow for building up the resources or financial support that may be required for full project implementation;

■ Or offering to do a **"pilot"** project, which in essence provides a trial period for your project that may address any skepticism or concerns and objections that government officials might have about the project.

Allowing a trial time to experience a project, may bring with it support for your project down the road.

■ Another approach may be to formulate the solution by simply offering a **"first step,"** in its implementation, and thereby creating political traction and building momentum for the ultimate solution you want to see implemented.

1st STEP

GET EXPERT SUPPORT AND ADVICE & DRAFT A READY-TO-ADOPT SOLUTION

Now it's time to put pen to paper (figuratively speaking) and begin drafting a constructive proposal

A constructive proposal will form the basis for any presentation you make to a public body for adoption of your proposed solution. And when you share it with friends and other citizens concerned about your issue, it can generate public support for your solution.

The first draft of your proposal should start out as a brief report (2 to 3 pages at most) that you can share with experts and professionals who can furnish additional information to help you finalize your proposal and increase the chances of its successful adoption.

The Initial Report should include:

1- The details of the current policy from the response to your public records request that demonstrates the past and/or present efforts of local government officials to address the issue and any positive elements of the current policy worth keeping;

2- Information about your proposed solution, especially its evidence of success and how you think it can fit in your city, town, or county.

This includes the information you gathered in your evidence-based research about the history or background of the issue in general and as it pertains to your community in particular. Include examples of the solution working in other places and explain why it should work in your community or county;

3- Your cost analysis. This includes any cost saving or information you got from reviewing your city, town or county's budget, such as how funds currently allocated to address this issue are being used or other possible sources of funding.

Share your report with professionals and experts who are knowledgeable about local government and your issue who can help you analyze and evaluate your proposed solution.

These individuals may be members of your community with significant knowledge of the issue and/or firsthand accounts and experiences in working in the field or in serving in government positions.

FOR EXAMPLE, you might seek advice by speaking with the City or County Administrator; or a respected retired government official; or a local attorney.

Connect with professors at law schools and universities who have expertise in local government matters, or experts at state associations of mayors, or other local officials or county officials.

You might also find helpful information on the National Solutions Sharing platform found on The Citizens Campaign's website at: **www.thecitizenscampaign.org**.

Incorporating any feedback or additional information you receive from consulting with professionals and expert sources leads to the last two components of a constructive proposal:

4- determining which public body has the authority to take the actions you propose

5- crafting your solution into a ready-to-adopt format. These two factors are related and important!

FOR EXAMPLE, if your solution requires that a new law be adopted, your proposed solution would take the form of an ordinance and would be directed to your local officials, i.e., A) the Mayor and City Council, or B) the County Commission or Council – the governing bodies with the authority to enact laws for our towns, cities and counties.

On the other hand, Executive Orders are usually issued by the chief executive- this usually means the mayor or county executive. Also, different public bodies have different areas of decision-making power under the law.

THUS, IT IS CRITICAL TO CHECK THAT LOCAL GOVERNMENT HAS JURISDICTION IN THE AREA OF YOUR CONCERN.

FOR EXAMPLE, if you are concerned about speed limits being too high on area roads, you need to check to see whether they are local or state roads.
(Please see chapter 1 describing the major decision-making arenas in local government.)

So here is another time to consult with professionals and experts in local government for advice on the form of your solution and the appropriate forum for considering it.

This is really a necessity.

It *insures* that you're not wasting your time appearing before the wrong public body.

To make sure you are presenting to the right officials, other ways of determining the right forum *include* checking the documents you received from your records request to see which public body adopted the current policy, or just asking local officials.

Also, experts and knowledgeable professionals in local government can be found at law schools and universities in your area or at state associations of local government officials.

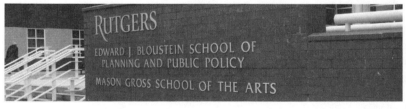

YOUR INITIAL REPORT SHOULD NOW BE DEVELOPED INTO A FINAL CONSTRUCTIVE PROPOSAL WITH THE FOLLOWING COMPONENTS:

1- State the issue or problem for which you will be proposing a solution

2- Provide background information about the issue or problem, including the fact-based reasons for addressing the problem in the manner which you will propose.

This is where you state your findings resulting from your evidence-based research, public records requests, and cost analysis.

3- Propose a solution that aims to rectify the issue, preferably in persuasive language that highlights the benefits of the solution

4- Identify the government entity responsible for implementing the proposed action.

5- Indicate how the solution will be enacted, i.e., the form of the solution:
- ordinance,
- resolution,
- executive order, etc.

6- Attach the legal form of your solution, if one is available from your research,
- or from The Citizens Campaign's National Solutions Sharing platform,
- or if you have one you drafted with the help of experts.
- Make sure the legal form of your solution includes recognition of the positive aspects of the existing policy.

PRESENTING YOUR SOLUTION FOR ADOPTION

Now that you have found and developed your solution, you should start preparing for the meeting where you will be presenting it. Besides the members of the governmental body that will be hearing your proposal, ask yourself who else might have an interest in your proposal. Reach out to those individuals and groups.

FOR EXAMPLE, if your solution is going to be before the Board of Education, then it might be helpful to seek the support of the teachers union and/or the PTO. Tell them about your proposal, the evidence that it works and is cost effective, and let them know you plan to present it for adoption. Ask them if they have any suggestions and, if they are supportive, to come to the hearing and speak in favor of your proposal.

You can also share information about your proposal and the upcoming hearing with friends on social media and you might notify traditional media outlets as well.

FINALLY, if you think that the general public would be broadly supportive, you might request that the specific hearing date, time and place, with a brief explanation of your solution, be included on a community calendar in your local newspaper.

Of course, before you arrange to go to a meeting and make your presentation, you should gather information about the meeting times, dates and locations for the public body that will be considering your proposal.

Becoming familiar with the rules and the conduct of the public body which will be hearing your proposal is a very important component of planning for your presentation. There are two important ways to accomplish this:

FIRST, you should consider attending a meeting or two in advance of the meeting where you will be making your presentation.

■ When you go to such meetings, you should arrive *early.* This will give you an opportunity to meet with government officials before the meeting starts and maybe chat, and you can pick up a copy of the meeting agenda so you know how meeting matters are prioritized.

You can also speak with the clerk or secretary to ask if there's a sign-up sheet or any other information that may be helpful for the public to know.

In any event, whether at a prep meeting or the meeting for your presentation, introduce yourself to public officials and to any media people covering the meeting and say hi to your neighbors and other citizens you may know who are attending.

SECOND, but equally important is to obtain a copy of the rules for citizen input at the meetings from the city clerk, or secretary to your school board, or look online.

■ While we know that most city, town and county governments provide citizens with time to speak during meetings, you should also know that there are almost always rules in place governing this process.
FOR EXAMPLE:

– Do citizens have to indicate in advance that they want to speak at the meeting?

– When during the meeting can citizens speak?

– Are there time limits for speaking?

If citizens only get to speak towards the end of a meeting, you might have to make special arrangements for child care or other matters.

It is also useful to know how long you are permitted to speak so that you can tailor your presentation to fit the allotted time period.

■ Sometimes citizens can team up to make a presentation in parts when the complete presentation can't fit into a single citizen's allowed time period.

■ If you have to sign up at the beginning or sometime in advance of the meeting, *make sure you're on the meeting agenda to speak*.

■ Additionally, if your city, town or county council or other public body limits comments to the agenda items which are up for a vote or discussion, you should request, in advance, permission to make your own proposal. Experience has shown that such requests are usually granted.

In summary, it is always to your advantage to be familiar with the usual process and procedures of the meetings and hearings at which you will be presenting – you will feel more comfortable if you are prepared and know the lay of the land!

BEING PROPERLY PREPARED ALSO MEANS DRESSING APPROPRIATELY.

Business attire is always a good choice, as that is what you'd expect council or board members to be wearing, and it is a fact that impressions are created even before we begin speaking.

Thus, if you dress appropriately, you and your presentation will have a better chance of being taken seriously.

NEXT, after you've taken the lay of the land and know the rules for engagement, you should prepare to deliver a respectful, constructive, and therefore, politically effective presentation.

ONE OF THE MOST IMPORTANT FACTORS TO CONSIDER IN PREPARING TO DELIVER YOUR PRESENTATION IS THE PRINCIPLE OF MUTUAL RESPECT

The most *persuasive* presentation will be a *respectful* one. Conducting a respectful presentation necessarily means using a no-blame strategy. If you rely on a respectful, no-blame approach, you will set the proper tone for the presentation and increase your chances for a more positive and successful outcome.

Be respectful at all times, whether you are asking a question or making a statement, even when you are challenged or others are rude or dismissive to you. *Remember, if you give respect, you can command respect.*

- Begin by thanking the officials for giving you the opportunity to speak.

- Then lead off your presentation with a review of the current policy you found using public records requests and your personal inquiries.

- Identify and praise the parts you agree with and go on to say that the solution you are presenting will positively build upon these aspects.

- Make sure you compliment the public officials and any other appropriate officials on the progress they've made so far in the issue area your solution is impacting.

It is important to note that here again, the no-blame strategy means you do not criticize public officials who may disagree with your proposal, but rather that you find common ground in the current policy or at least recognize common goals and a belief that differences can be worked out.

The good news is, however, that it is difficult for a public official to express disagreement with a proposed solution that is:

1- evidence based (you have shown that the solution has worked in places similar to your own community),

2- that it is cost effective, (you have shown that it will not have a negative impact on your local government's budget),

3- and you are utilizing your no-blame strategy exercising civility and respect throughout the process of finding and presenting your solution.

HERE IS A SAMPLE
PRESENTATION FORMAT BEFORE A CITY COUNCIL

FIRST: *Begin with respectful opening remarks*
"Mayor _____

(or if the mayor is not in attendance, **Council President_____**),
**members of the Council, my name is _____
and I reside at _____.
I appreciate the opportunity to speak to you tonight and
to hear your thoughts on what I hope you will consider
to be a constructive proposal."**

SECOND: Recognize any past and present efforts of the
council to deal with the issue you are speaking about. Showing
appreciation for their efforts will help them appreciate your
effort.

**THIRD: Make your proposal with a realistic request for
action**. Your proposal should include a request that specific
action be taken with regard to the solution you are proposing.
Asking the council to consider your proposal and take a
practical "**first step**" is a constructive and politically effective
approach to doing this.

FOURTH: Make closing remarks with a clincher. Not only
should you request that action be taken, you should ask for
the specific time frame for any action proposed.

———■■■———

This will avoid the situation that citizens often find themselves
in after making a proposal, even a proposal that is delivered
intelligently and responsibly - *not knowing or being uncertain
about what the public body thinks about the proposal and
what if any action will be taken.*

*If not asked to specify how and when a response will be given,
the public body will merely say thank you and may just move
to the next item on their agenda.*

RESPECTFUL PURSUIT
TO IMPLEMENTATION OF YOUR SOLUTION

Follow-up after your presentation of a proposal is always needed. It would be rare indeed if a proposal is adopted at its initial presentation, and even in such an instance, a follow-up thank you to members of the public body would be in order.

Here are some useful pointers in exercising respectful pursuit so that positive action on your proposal is the end result:

■ If at the hearing, your proposal is referred to a professional or subcommittee for further discussion or review, e.g., the town's lawyer or administrator or subcommittee of the council, *always* ask the following:

"May I please ask for what purpose (if not already stated) this matter is being referred to the subcommittee or professional and whether a report will be forthcoming, and if so, when?"

Additional tactics of respectful pursuit include:

■ **Offer to meet individually with Council members** and/or city/town/county professionals to discuss the proposal and possible ways to move it forward – and if an official makes a commitment to do something, always ask what time frame they feel comfortable with for fulfilling the commitment.

■ **After meeting with an official**
Follow-up with a written thank you mentioning the commitments made by the official – the time frame they indicated they were comfortable with for fulfilling the commitment – and if it's an elected official who indicates that a department head or other staff person will act on the commitment, then copy that person on the thank you note as well. It's always a good idea to thank those people that offer assistance, including public officials and government workers; cultivating various sources is always useful.

■ **If there is a concern** about the scale of your proposal – or about inadequate resources to implement it, offer a compromise that might include implementing your proposal in phases or as a pilot program.

■ **Seek a resolution** or other recommendation of your solution from an appropriate city, county or school district board or committee.

■ **Garner community support** for your proposal from non-profit organizations, businesses, government employee associations or recognized leaders in your community; – these individuals and entities can write letters of support, – can show support by their presence at government meetings, – and can advocate for your solution among their own constituents.

■ **Demonstrating that there are significant numbers** of individual citizens in the community that actively support your proposal is another way to pursue its adoption. You can bring your friends and neighbors together to show support for your proposal by personally inviting them to a meeting at your home, or other convenient location, posting flyers, ringing doorbells and the like.

- **Enlist your neighborhood political party representative** in support of your proposal. In most states, there are local Democratic and Republican Party committee-people at the neighborhood level as well as town and county party chairs. These folks often have influence with the elected officials of their party and as a result, it is helpful to get them involved actively pushing your proposal. (To find out more information about the specifics of the political party structure in your state and local area, visit the following websites:

    Association of State Democratic Committees at:
    https://asdc.democrats.org/state-parties/

    Republican Party State Leadership at:
    https://gop.com/leaders/states/)

- **Use conventional and social media channels** to spread the word about your proposal and to have others publicly indicate their support for your proposal; you can speak about your proposal to a reporter or editor of a local paper (both in print and online versions); You should also ask your social media contacts to spread the word about your proposal to their friends and contacts in an ever-widening circle of friends.

■ **Use communication tools and resources** to follow-up with government officials and build support for your proposal.

Elected officials should pay close attention to the mail, phone calls and emails they receive. You can conduct a letter-writing, phone call and email campaign reaching out to them.

Personal letters in someone's own words can be very effective. If you are contacting a councilperson, mayor or county elected official and live in the official's voting district, when calling or emailing, always identify yourself as a constituent and give an address.

■ **You can create a blog** that focuses on the issue and solution you are proposing and solicit comments.

■ If it is legal in your town or county, you may use **Initiative and Referendum**. **I & R** should only be used as a last resort because it is very time consuming and may invite a legal challenge.

"Government is not inherently good or bad.
It is a tool. And how it works
depends upon how well we use it."

– James J. Florio
Former Governor, State of New Jersey

THE CITIZENS CAMPAIGN
NO-BLAME PROBLEM SOLVING GUIDE

10 KEY STEPS
TO GET RESULTS

In years of experience working with citizens and government officials, I have tried to develop a straightforward process that citizens can use to help them find solutions to the issues and problems they identify as important to them and their hometowns.

I have laid out this process in a compact "No-Blame Problem Solving Guide" which sets forth 10 key steps, beginning with identifying an issue, searching for and drafting a solution, and finally, getting it adopted.

Each step involves certain aspects which should be considered, some requiring more time and attention than others. And while you may be passionate about an issue facing your community, it is often more effective to work with others, your friends and neighbors, in trying to address the problem and explore solutions.

The "10 Step" allows for, and in fact encourages, you to work together with others toward the betterment of your community. It is the Problem Solving Guide that is used by Civic Trustees and that has helped citizens pass over 300 local laws incorporating their chosen solutions. (Please go to chapter 9 to learn about becoming a Civic Trustee and/or creating a Civic Trust in your community).

1

STEP Identify your issue focus

DRILL DOWN TO A SPECIFIC PROBLEM YOU CARE ABOUT

❏ Engage in bottom-up conversations with your fellow citizens to identify consensus passions about specific issues.

❏ Prioritize identified issues. Considerations may include: internal support (within the group), expected external support (from community and/or administration), timing, difficulty of the problem, scope of problem, etc.

❏ Drill down the issue(s) to a discernable problem in the chosen issue area that you believe you can tackle with a doable solution.

2
STEP Submit an Open Records Request
FIND OUT HOW THE CURRENT POLICY WORKS

___

❏ First, investigate what your city/town/county/school district is currently doing to address your priority issue by exploring the city/town/county/school district website, media coverage, or making phone calls to the appropriate office.

❏ Dig deeper by preparing a public records request of documents creating the current policy for submission either to the City government, county government, or the school district. Remember that you are requesting copies of existing records (e.g. resolutions, ordinances, written policies and procedures), so be as specific as possible.

❏ Find and submit the public records request form/letter to the appropriate party. Sample request letters for your state can be downloaded at https://www.nfoic.org/organizations/state-sample-foia-request-letters. (Please note: Request forms or instructions are often available on the city, town, school district, or county government's website.)

3

STEP Conduct Evidence-Based research

FIND PROVEN SUCCESSFUL POLICIES

❏ An internet search is the best place to start! Look up your priority issue to find policies with evidence of success in communities similar to your own. Look for news articles, policy papers, or websites on the topic.

❏ Dig deeper. Look into academic institutions, including university departments and centers that specialize in the issue area.

❏ Call or check websites of associations whose focus is local government or who deal with your issue area (e.g. Here are a few selected examples from around the nation: Michigan Municipal League, Colorado Association of School Boards, Georgia Economic Developers Association, The New Jersey Association of Environmental Commissions. Your state should have similar organizations.)

❏ Review The Citizens Campaign's Solutions Sharing Platform which contains evidence-based solutions previously developed by other Citizens Campaign participants and the experts from its Law & Policy Task Force.

4
STEP Shape your Solution

TAILOR YOUR SOLUTION TO FIT LOCAL
CIRCUMSTANCES & BUILD UPON THE CURRENT POLICY

❏ Dig deeper to determine what it took to implement your researched solution. How long did it take to put into effect? Were staff reassigned to implement it? Was any staff training required? Was the budget amended to reallocate funds for the new policy?

❏ Review the current policy that you seek to modify or replace and determine if there are any parts of it worth keeping as is or with slight modification.

❏ Consider any feedback or concerns expressed by elected officials or government staff about your proposed policy.

❏ Now shape your solution to address the information you've collected in the reviews referenced above. The more your solution fits with and positively builds on the current policy, and the more it takes into consideration the feedback of government officials and the hurdles of implementation, the better chance of it being adopted and successfully implemented.

STEP Make sure it's Cost Effective

A PRACTICAL SOLUTION IS BUDGET NEUTRAL
– OR BETTER

❏ From evidence you gathered in your research, determine whether there will be costs involved in implementing your solution such as administrative costs, staff time, etc., or whether it will be cost-neutral (or better yet – cost saving).

❏ If there are costs involved, look at your city, school district or county's budget to determine whether your solution would be covered by a particular line item, and if not, whether there are any other areas from which savings could be sufficient to offset the costs of your solution.

❏ If the solution is not covered by the city/county/school district budget and you cannot find any offsetting budget cuts, come up with alternative funding sources. Look for grants, consider crowd funding, etc. This is especially important if there are start-up costs that will disappear or be offset by savings in future budgets.

STEP **Do the Doable**

THE ART OF PHASING
AND PILOTING

❏ It's often better to start smaller and gain traction in order to build support and find funds for the overall solution.

❏ "Phasing" is a good tactic (implementing the solution in steps or phases), especially when full funding is not available.

❏ "Pilot" projects are also useful when there is skepticism about your solution or when you need to show that start-up costs will be offset by savings in future budgets.

7
STEP Get Support from Experts
SUCCESSFUL PRACTITIONERS CAN PROVIDE LEGAL
AND STRATEGIC ADVICE

❏ Draft a brief (1 to 2 page) report that includes information about: (1) the response to your public records request; (2) your proposed solution, evidence of its success, and how you think it can fit in your city or county; and (3) your cost analysis.

❏ After completing the report, you may consider seeking further advice from experts or professionals in local/county/ school district government, or professors and experts at law schools and universities, or experts at specialized associations or organizations, who could review the report and assist with your analysis and the further development of your proposal, including the preferred legal form for adoption. Options include ordinances, resolutions, executive orders, and administrative policies or procedures.

❏ Incorporate changes suggested by the expert(s) or conduct any suggested additional research.

8

STEP Present a Ready-to-Adopt Solution
PRESENTING A DRAFT LAW CALLS FOR A VOTE

❏ Get a copy of the legal document that created your chosen successful solution. It is a good starting point for implementing the solution in your town.

❏ Work with a volunteer lawyer or your town or county's attorney, if supportive, to incorporate your chosen solution into the preferred legal format. Options include ordinances, resolutions, executive orders, and administrative policies or procedures.

❏ Make sure to include language recognizing the positive aspects of your town or county's existing policy and any recent, related initiatives in the draft of the law to enact your solution.

STEP Make a *Respectful* presentation

IF YOU GIVE RESPECT, YOU CAN COMMAND RESPECT

❏ Dress respectfully and address officials respectfully.

❏ Review your town or county's current policy and find what parts you agree with. Then come in complimenting the officials on that part(s) of the current policy and offer to build upon it.

❏ In any event, when presenting to the public body, compliment them on the progress they've made so far in your issue area.

❏ When speaking to the media, ***do not criticize public officials*** who disagree with your proposal.
Be understanding of their positions and concerns and ***express confidence that you can work things out.***

10
STEP Respectful Pursuit

HOW TO *DIPLOMATICALLY* PUSH FOR ADOPTION

❏ If your solution is deferred for further discussion or review by government committees or experts, say, *"Please, may I ask to whom is this proposal being referred and when can we expect a response from this public body?"*

❏ When meeting with an official who makes a commitment to do something to advance your solution, always ask what time frame they feel comfortable with for fulfilling the commitment.

❏ After meeting with an elected official, follow up with a written thank you note mentioning the commitments made by the official and the time frame they indicated they were comfortable with for fulfilling the commitment. If it's an elected official who indicates that a department head or other staff person will act on the commitment, copy that person on the thank you note.

❏ Consult legal and policy experts to see if there is a way to implement the solution without governmental approval.

❏ Keep your solution in the picture by using social media and conventional media and keep it "No-Blame."

❏ Ask for support from people and organizations in your community.

❏ Seek a resolution, or other support recommending your solution, from an appropriate board or commission.

❏ Try an Executive Order (if legal) if there aren't enough votes for adopting an ordinance.

❏ Seek support from a government employees' union.

❏ Wait until election time and seek sponsorship from an incumbent who is a candidate (presidential and gubernatorial election times are preferable).

❏ If you meet with continuing opposition from the decision-maker, offer a compromise, if possible, such as a pilot or phased-in approach.

❏ Use **Initiative and Referendum** if that is an option available in your city, county or school district. Initiative and Referendum should only be used as a last resort.

CHAPTER SEVEN

MEDIA LITERACY IN THE SEARCH FOR SOLUTIONS

Technology enhances your ability to *find* successful solutions using search engines such as Google or Bing and *share* them with your fellow citizens on social media sites such as Facebook and Twitter.

However, searching online isn't without its shortcomings. Information posing as fact has proliferated so widely that even the most discerning eye can be fooled. Poorly written articles by unqualified journalists and stories written to purposely misinform run rampant on the internet.

YOUR CREDIBILITY RESTS ON THE VERACITY OF YOUR RESEARCH

If the research you present to a governing body, a journalist, or the public is misinformation, your credibility will be severely damaged. Fortunately, there are a number of ways to avoid getting tricked...

It's important to approach any information you uncover with a critical eye. But how do you do this when even the most reputable sources may contain information that was misreported? The following tips are some of the ways you can evaluate the information you plan to use in your research.

FOREMOST, ENSURE THAT THE SOURCE/PUBLICATION YOU'RE READING IS CREDIBLE

Look for sites with a history of publishing credible information that are often cited by established organizations, such as major news outlets, think tanks, academic articles, etc.

- Look to see if the site you are researching publishes corrections to stories. No publication, no matter how reputable, has a perfect record of accuracy. Retractions and corrections show their editors value facts.

- Find out if the site is referenced favorably by established opinion leaders, either nationally or in your state and community. Do a search on Twitter to see what kind of conversations are taking place about the site you're looking at and if it is trusted.

Snopes.com maintains a list of websites known to promote misleading news.

CONSIDER THE EXPERTISE OF THE STORY'S AUTHOR

Authors have varied experiences as journalists and experts on any given topic. Sometimes news organizations assign inexperienced journalists to beats that require specialized knowledge, like court reporters and science writers. Do some research into their backgrounds — most have a Linkedin or Twitter account— to help evaluate their experience. See if their reporting experience or academic history exhibits a competency in their beat.

CONSIDER THE SOURCES THE STORY USES AS SUPPORTING INFORMATION

Online stories often contain links to primary documents, other news stories, personal testimonies, or statements on behalf of an institution.

- If a quoted source contains a link, check to see if the linked story corresponds to what the story is reporting.
- If the source is a quoted individual, do a web search to find other stories quoting this person, find a company bio on the individual, or look for their social media profiles. Anonymous sourcing is a standard practice in journalism to protect a source who may be risking retaliation for talking on the record.

However, sometimes individuals remain anonymous to avoid accountability and to provide cover when passing false information. When researching solutions, your evidence will have more impact if you're working from primary sources rather than from secondary or third-hand sources.

BE SKEPTICAL OF SENSATIONAL HEADLINES

Headlines are often purposefully provocative or vague to compel the reader to click on the link. This is because the business model of most online news websites' is derived from pay-for-performance advertising – the more impressions an article gets when people click on it, the more money the organization raises from the ads displayed on the page. Chances are the story is more benign than the headline implies.

Remember, the headline is not the full story. Take the time to read the whole story and see if it is consistent with the  headline before drawing a conclusion based on the headline alone. Make sure when you share a story on social media the headline accurately reflects what the story is reporting, or be sure to note that the headline is misleading but the story still contains solid and useful information.

NOTE THE DATE THE STORY WAS PUBLISHED

When you find articles while researching your issue, ensure that the date of the article reflects contemporary events. If the article is over a year old, there may be a chance that there is further reporting that strengthens or weakens the points highlighted in the article. Do further research to see if this is the case.

When sharing on social media, the timeliness of a story is important to consider especially if it references a current event. Sometimes people share older articles that have the unintended consequence of distorting current events. People sharing old news may be mistaken to think it relates to a current situation (e.g., a story about a municipality bonding for a new capital project despite the fact that the municipality is currently facing a budget crisis; the story is from several years prior and has nothing to do with the current budget situation). Before sharing on social media, make sure the story was published recently enough that it reflects current events accurately.

FIND EXPERT OPINION

It is not unusual that the evidence you have found on your topic area is too complex to understand without having specialized knowledge. Documents like legal opinions, architectural plans, housing plans, and environmental commission reports may require expert advice.

PERHAPS THE HARDEST ASPECT TO OVERCOME IS ONE'S OWN BIAS

This is more widely known as '**confirmation bias**' – the tendency to interpret new evidence as confirmation of one's existing beliefs or theories.

Personal bias is also the hardest to identify since people are reluctant to doubt their own beliefs. Counter this by remaining skeptical of stories that confirm your worldview. If you read a story about misconduct involving a public figure you already do not trust, do not automatically assume the story to be accurate.

Remember, the no-blame approach requires that you get past your personal biases when researching and sharing solutions. When you are not looking to place blame on a person or particular party, your personal bias can be set aside and your full attention can be directed to evaluating the evidence.

CHAPTER

8

SERVING CITIZEN SOLUTIONS CIVIC TRUSTEE

Powerful Roles for Citizen Problem Solvers

Citizens who wish to engage in public service but don't want to dive into the world of campaign politics with its heavy fundraising demands, its blame-game personal attacks, and its major demands on time, can still engage in leadership service without having to run for public office.   There are four ways to do so:

- Serving as a Civic Trustee
- Serving as a Solutions Advocate
- Serving in an Appointed Government Office
- Serving as a Neighborhood Political Party Representative

SERVICE AS A CIVIC TRUSTEE

The most powerful, yet convenient, non-elected opportunity for public service is the position of Civic Trustee, a position facilitated by The Citizens Campaign. Information about qualifications and the rights and responsibilities of a Civic Trustee is available at www.TheCitizensCampaign.org. Civic Trustees are a new force for strengthening your community's ability to tackle tough issues. They are committed to identifying evidence-based, cost effective solutions to the serious problems facing their cities' and towns', and to advance and implement such solutions with a no-blame approach. In this role, Civic Trustees embody the values of unselfish service, civility and pragmatism.

Civic Trustees begin service by taking a pledge to

"leave their community and country better than they found them by pursuing practical solutions instead of just pointing out problems and assigning blame."

Practical solutions are those that:

1- are based on evidence of success in other cities and towns;

2- cost-effective in that they do not increase the tax burden;

3- beneficial to the community as a whole rather than a special interest,

4- and are advanced in a no-blame manner.

Civic Trustees who receive training and follow the proven no-blame problem solving approach in pursuing practical solutions, can access free expert support from The Citizens Campaign's Law and Policy Task Force of lawyers, former government officials and other experts in local law, policy and policy implementation.

CIVIC TRUSTEES COME TOGETHER IN CIVIC TRUSTS THAT ARE ESTABLISHED IN THEIR HOMETOWNS

Civic Trusts provide the opportunity for Civic Trustees to "meet" in monthly "solution sessions," where they work together in a no-blame environment to identify the issues they believe are most pressing in their community and then research and advance workable solutions.

Hometown Civic Trusts are comprised of:

- 12 to 24 Trustees, depending on the community's population size.

- Trustees serve for terms of one year and can serve up to three consecutive terms.

- Residents and other stakeholders in the community become members of the Trust based on their demonstrated leadership capacity; that is, they have been successful in getting others to work together to accomplish a goal, and they have a passionate commitment to their city.

- They must also have the time available to work with their fellow Trustees by participating in the monthly "solution sessions."

On the following page is a sample application form to become a Civic Trustee. An application form can also be found in The Citizens Campaign Power Portal.

CIVIC TRUST

THE QUALITIES OF CIVIC TRUSTEESHIP

The Civic Trusteeship Application provides you with an opportunity to tell us a little about yourself

Some things to consider as you complete this very brief application:

Leadership is demonstrated in many ways. You don't need to hold office or run a company to be considered a leader. Civic Trustees are leaders in their community who have been successful in helping other people accomplish a goal. This sort of leadership can come from coaching or being captain of a team, starting a club, or managing a community project. There is no one way to lead, so please share your unique experience with us.

Civic Trustees have a special relationship with their city. Whether you live, work, or attend school in the city, all Civic Trustees share a passion and commitment to making their city stronger than it is today.

We look forward to getting to know you.

1- What is your full name?

_____

2- What is the best phone number to reach you during weekday business hours?

_____

3- What is your home address?

_____

CITY_____ ZIP_____

4- What is the best email address to reach you?

_____

5- Are you applying to serve in a specific Civic Trust?

_____

6- What is your relationship with Your City?

- ❑ I live here
- ❑ I work here
- ❑ I go/went to school here
- ❑ I grew up here

7- Are you on social media?

- ❑ Yes   ❑ No

Please list all of your social media names for Facebook and Twitter.

_____

_____

_____

_____

8- Please indicate which issue areas you are most interested in: (Pick up to three)

- ❑ Education
- ❑ Public Safety
- ❑ Economic Development
- ❑ Government Efficiency & Waste Cutting
- ❑ Environment
- ❑ Citizen Empowerment
- ❑ Other:

9- In becoming a Civic Trustee, I pledge to leave my community better than I found it by:

- ❑ Searching for solutions
  instead of simply pointing out problems

- ❑ Working on solutions that are "doable"
  -- that are cost effective and based on evidence
  of success

- ❑ Pursuing the adoption of solutions
  with a no-blame approach

A New Jersey Civic Trust Forum on the solutions for CSOs (combined sewer overflow)

Civic Trusts also provide the opportunity and structure for arranging No-Blame Solutions Forums for community decision-makers. Solutions Forums bring experts and professionals together with city decision-makers to discuss evidence based solutions in issue areas that are being explored by Civic Trustees.

Bringing their town's decision makers together in a no-blame environment, and *exposing them to evidence based solutions* offered by experts, is a powerful way for Civic Trustees to help put their community on the path of practical problem solving.

A New Jersey Civic Trust meeting

Civic Trustee Darren "Freedom" Green guest lecturing on Power Civics at American History High School, Newark NJ

Civic Trustees are also involved in the recruitment of citizens to public service by being guest speakers at high school civics classes and college Power Civics Forums. In the role of guest speaker, Civic Trustees offer their example and their knowledge of citizen problem solving to motivate their fellow citizens to get in the game of bettering their community. Trustee guest speakers also recruit new members for their city's Civic Trust, creating a continuing source of new Civic Trustees and future community leadership.

Lastly and quite importantly, Civic Trustees share their solutions with citizens in towns and cities across the country causing their local actions to have national impact.

If you are interested in public service as a Civic Trustee and/ or in forming a Civic Trust in your community, you will find all the necessary information online at The Citizens Campaign's website.

SERVICE AS A SOLUTIONS ADVOCATE

Another powerful role you can take on to advance no-blame problem solving in your community is as a Solutions Advocate. Solutions Advocates are citizens who find and promote evidence based, cost-effective, successful solutions to decision makers and the general public.

Bringing such practical solutions to government officials, the media, and your fellow citizens, can impact and change the political and governmental climate from one focused on who has the power, to one focused on who has the solutions.

When our elected officials are provided with a constant stream of practical workable solutions, they will have less time to point fingers and assign blame because their attention will be directed to responding to solutions. *It is this discussion of solutions which elevates the political dialogue and makes our government work.*

Solutions Advocates bring a positive focus to governance in three ways:

FIRST, they share their solutions with their elected officials and fellow citizens through social media;

SECOND, they send their solutions research to members of the media who are working on related stories;   and

THIRD, they write letters to the editor that showcase the successful solution.

YOUR TOWN'S FACEBOOK GROUP

Facebook Groups may be the easiest and most efficient way to promote a practical solution in your community. Many towns have town-focused Facebook Groups where residents discuss current events and issues affecting their community.

During the course of your research you may find news articles from other communities that successfully implemented policies which address a similar issue facing your town.

- Share the story within the group and include a short write up on how the solution could be applicable to your community.

- Also, consider encouraging group members to share this with community leaders and offer any relevant information they might have about the proposed solution.

FACEBOOK GROUPS have the added benefit of allowing you to post documents such as PDFs and Word documents – something you cannot share in a regular Facebook post. Document sharing can be useful if you want to distribute government documents you received from a public records request, or may have found elsewhere online or through other sources.

Oftentimes, members of the governing body and school board monitor these groups to see what is being discussed in town, sometimes even posting something of their own.

Your solution may catch the attention of one of these officials who may ask for more information or offer to introduce it to their colleagues.

DEVELOP A RELATIONSHIP WITH YOUR LOCAL NEWS EDITOR/REPORTER

Local news organizations are scaling back their staff affecting editors' and reporters' ability to research and amplify stories on local issues. And since the business model of many news outlets is to draw clicks to drive up advertising revenue, stories tend to focus heavily on controversies rather than solutions.

The saying "If it bleeds, it leads" is as relevant today as it has ever been. As a Solutions Advocate, you can help your local reporter by providing your evidence-based research on topics they are covering. Find stories in their  publications that could benefit from your research and forward such information to them with a short cover note explaining how your research could benefit further articles on the subject.

WRITE LETTERS TO THE EDITOR/OPINION PIECES

Letters TO THE Editor If you are politely declined by an editor or reporter or receive no response, consider writing a letter to the editor for publication, referencing a recent article on the issue and describing your solution in the letter.

In most print newspapers, letters to the editor run on the same page as the editorials, and public officials tend to monitor them closely. Generally, letters should be no more than 200 words. It's a good idea to always check with the newspaper to see if they have a word limit, and if there are any other requirements for submission.

Another effective way to reach community leaders and the general public is through submission of an opinion piece. As a Solutions Advocate, your opinion piece would reflect the fact that there's a solution to the issue that is the subject of articles and coverage by the paper.

Most daily print newspapers have an opinion page that includes syndicated columnists, the paper's own opinion columnists, and guest opinion columns. Traditionally, the limit for a guest opinion column is usually around 600 words. Here too, before submitting an opinion piece, you should check with the paper to find out what their word limit is and any other requirements they may have for a guest submission.

The best way to get a sense of how to write an opinion piece is to read the opinion pages of newspapers in which you are interested. This will give you a sense of how opinion pieces are structured and what kinds the newspapers tend to publish.

■ Submitting your piece with an attached cover letter that briefly makes the case for why you think the newspaper should publish it increases your chances of success. The cover letter can include a brief explanation of no-blame problem solving and the importance of focusing decision-making on evidence based, cost effective solutions. As always, follow-up with the opinion page editor and any other relevant contacts to also increase your chances of publication.

And as you work to develop relationships with reporters and news media personnel through your efforts as a Solutions Advocate, you may become positioned to suggest story ideas to them. This would be an opportunity to suggest writing an article about other solutions being advanced in your town.

SERVE AS A SOLUTIONS ADVOCATE FOR A CIVIC TRUST

Solutions Advocates also may choose to become Civic Trustees. They assist their fellow Civic Trustees with promotion and implementation of Trustee proposals by using social media to build a base of support for adoption of the proposed solution.

Solutions Advocates may work in an independent way, however, they can have greater impact when they employ their skills in a team effort with trained no-blame problem solvers.

SERVICE IN AN APPOINTED LOCAL GOVERNMENT OFFICE

There are dozens of appointed leadership positions in local government boards and commissions and on task forces of local school boards. Nearly all municipal and county governments throughout the nation have a wide range of volunteer boards and commissions that deal with a variety of issues and that provide opportunities for public service.

FOR EXAMPLE,

- for those interested in the physical development of the city, there usually are zoning and planning boards and historic preservation, open space and environmental commissions;

- for those interested in quality of life improvements there are recreation and human relations commissions, economic development boards and arts councils;

- for those interested in specific constituent and enforcement issues there are parking and housing authorities, youth councils and health commissions.

DECIDING WHERE TO SERVE:

So the first step in seeking an appointed position is to get a list or directory of the boards and commissions in your community. This listing is often available on your city/town/county's website. You can also check with the municipal or county clerk.

- It is important to check and see if there are any existing vacancies or terms expiring soon.

- Review the list and see which boards interest you.

- Check online or ask the clerk for a schedule of board meeting dates, times, and locations.
  Then determine if your schedule would permit you to attend.

APPLYING TO SERVE:

Check to see whether there is a formal application process for serving on the board or commission of your choice. If so, fill out and submit the application as directed. If there isn't an established process, write to the Chairperson of the board or commission and express your interest in serving.

PURSUING AN APPOINTMENT TO YOUR CHOSEN BOARD:

Find out who has the authority to make appointments to your chosen board and tell them that you applied or wrote to the Chairperson to express your interest in serving.

- Introduce yourself to government officials, including your elected representatives, and to political party leaders who may have sway in the appointment decision-making process. If you haven't yet done so, introduce yourself to the chair and members of the board you wish to be appointed to and express your interest in the work and service that they do.

- Attend board meetings regularly so you become a familiar presence. Take advantage of any opportunities to work with board members on any projects or events they are hosting in the community.

AFTER YOU'RE APPOINTED:

Understand the mission and goals of the board and how it is intended to serve the community by getting a copy of the resolution/ordinance/law that created the board or commission. It will state the purpose of the board and may describe the extent of its authority. Learn the rules of participation on your board by obtaining and reviewing the rules of procedure (also known as administrative codes). Pay special attention to the rules for placing an item on the board's agenda, as this is the procedure for bringing your solutions up for discussion and decision-making.

Exercise no-blame problem solving skills in carrying out your responsibilities as a board member and be guided by the principles of mutual respect and civil discourse in dealing with other board members and the general public.

Most importantly, become an effective board member and citizen leader by researching to find evidence based, cost effective solutions to issues or problems the board confronts.

NOTE: If no board or commission exists in your town that deals with the policy issues in which you are interested to better your community, you can develop a proposal to put before your mayor and council, school board or county government as the case may be, to establish a new board or task force.

Conduct research to find out if other towns have such boards and how they were established. Then get a copy of the ordinance or resolution establishing the board and prepare a presentation to your local council, school board or county government suggesting they create one. Remember to follow the No- Blame Problem Solving Guide to increase your chances of success in this endeavor!

SERVICE AS A NEIGHBORHOOD POLITICAL PARTY REPRESENTATIVE

Another way to serve your community is as a neighborhood political party representative, usually called a committeeman or woman or district leader.

The roles, responsibilities and rules that govern these grassroots party positions vary from state to state. Generally speaking, however, citizens in these neighborhood districts who are members with a party, elect committee-people at the primary elections to represent them in political party decision making.

The decisions made by neighborhood representatives are important ones, often having huge impact, such as
- the endorsement of candidates for public office,
- the establishment of the party's platform priorities for their town, i.e.,
  - the positions which party members who are elected to public office should focus on,
  - and the choice of their towns' party leaders.

To find out more information about how to become a committee-person or district leader in your local area, please visit the following websites:

Association of State Democratic Committees at: https://asdc.democrats.org/state-parties/

Republican Party State Leadership at: https://gop.com/leaders/states/

CIVIC TRUST

CHAPTER 9

PROBLEM SOLVER BENEFIT

THE CIVIC TRUST

A great opportunity to serve your community and your country

If you're reading this final chapter, I hope you've learned about becoming a No-Blame problem solver because in this role, you can serve your community in a new, exciting and positive way.

As participants in our democracy in today's world, we don't have to be limited to voting and protesting. Nor do we have to be candidates or government officials to play an active role in the decision-making processes of our government. We can work together to identify problems in our communities that need fixing, and find practical solutions – solutions that are evidence-based and cost-effective, and equally importantly, we can advance them in a No-Blame way to better ensure their adoption. We can do this best by becoming Civic Trustees and working together in a Civic Trust. Basically, here's how.

First, Civic Trusts are non-partisan and Trustees take a Civic Pledge to work toward the betterment of their communities and country.

THE CIVIC PLEDGE
I pledge to leave my community and country better than I found them by pursuing practical solutions instead of just pointing out problems and assigning blame.

Civic Trustees work together in a Civic Trust that operates and takes action in accordance with the principles of the Civic Pledge. A Trust is usually comprised of around 12 – 24 Trustees, depending on the size of the community. The Civic Trust meets on a monthly basis in "Solution Sessions" to work together using a proven problem solving method. Meetings are usually scheduled in the early evening, are approximately 2 hours in length and include a lite meal, making it convenient for Trustees coming from work. Locations for Trust meetings are also set for the convenience of their members in places such as schools, libraries, and community colleges.

THE TRUST'S ONGOING ACTIVITIES INCLUDE:

- Researching and advancing successful solutions that are working in other communities that could work in their own;
- Hosting No-Blame Solutions Forums for their city's elected officials and other decision-makers to meet and talk with experts and professionals on challenges facing the city in a No-Blame environment;
- Serving as guest speakers in high schools and colleges teaching Power Civics;
- Learning about successful solutions shared by Civic Trustees from other cities and towns;
- Recruiting other community stakeholders to serve as Civic Trustees to ensure sustainability of the Trust;
- Promoting citizen empowerment in their communities and among their friends.

Residents and other stakeholders that serve as Civic Trustees are truly carrying on traditions from the time of our forefathers.

They are acting as **'public citizens'** – that is they are advancing solutions to improve our government without having to run for public office. Their primary goal is selfless service to the community for its betterment.

 **Benjamin Franklin** (1706 -1790) one of the Founding Fathers of the United States, is a prime example – He's easily recognized for his many contributions to improving our society (political philosopher and one of the drafters of the Declaration of Independence, politician, civic activist, newspaper editor, founder of many civic organizations, creator of local fire departments, and founder of local schools and libraries...) *and he never was elected to public office!*

In today's world, Civic Trustees working together in Civic Trusts have won adoption of solutions to problems in the areas of climate change, police/community relations, and school discipline, to name a few. And through their work and example, Trustees are restoring the values of service and civility to America's political culture and pragmatism to our government.

In the great American tradition of the community barn-raising, we and our fellow citizens can put aside our judgments of each other and set to work to address the practical necessity of putting our government back on the path of practical problem solving.

If you would like to become a Civic Trustee
or want to help organize a Civic Trust in your community,
please visit The Citizens Campaign's website and look at
the Civic Trustee Handbook at the back of this manual.
www.thecitizenscampaign.org.

NOTE TO NON-CITIZENS

The United States is home to immigrants from all over the world and many have yet to become citizens. Non-citizens cannot vote in federal, state, or local elections nor can they run for office, but there are still many ways they can participate.

FOR EXAMPLE,

■ Non-citizens have the right to attend and be heard at meetings of the local power centers and have the right to information such as public records.

■ Non-citizens can volunteer on political campaigns and participate in non-profit groups.

Still, to completely participate in our democracy, it is important to gain citizenship. Some of the basic requirements include:

1- Lawful permanent residence in the United States for at least 5 years;

2- The ability to write, speak and understand basic English; and

3- Passing an exam on US history and government.

To apply for citizenship, you must fill out form N-400, which can be obtained from US Citizenship and Immigration Services at www.uscis.gov/n-400. Information on how to become a citizen and other immigration issues can also be found on this website.

HARRY S. POZYCKI

CHAIRMAN & FOUNDER ■ THE CITIZENS CAMPAIGN

Harry Pozycki is the Chairman and Founder of The Citizens Campaign, a non-partisan organization dedicated to bringing a solutions focus to our government and to restoring service, civility, and pragmatism to our political culture. Working as a full-time volunteer, with the help of former Harvard President, Derek Bok, and other Citizens Campaign board members, Harry assembled a team of government law experts and distinguished former government leaders. Together, they developed a "power platform" that teaches citizens evidence-based, public issue solving with a "no blame" strategy.

Expanding the reach and impact of citizen power, Harry then developed a program for creating community based Civic Trusts, where citizens, trained in no-blame problem solving, serve as Civic Trustees. Meeting in monthly "Solution Sessions," Civic Trustees work together to find practical solutions to the challenges facing their cities and our country.

In partnership with the University of Pennsylvania's Graduate School of Education, Harry also developed a high school curriculum known as *Power Civics*, and later an advanced college version. Combining the citizen leadership training of *Power Civics* with the public service opportunity of Civic Trusts, Harry recently launched the "Civic City" initiative, with a goal of expanding the problem-solving capacity of cities and, via sharing local solutions nationwide, the country.

For his substantial work and contributions in the civic arena, Harry received the New Jersey Governor's Jefferson Award for Civic Innovation and was recognized by the Philadelphia Inquirer as its Citizen of the Year.

In 2001, Harry brought all sides together to pass New Jersey's Open Public Records Act, which gives citizens access to government information so they can initiate constructive solutions without waiting for the political establishment. He was also the lead author of the Citizen Service Act and the Party Democracy Act, state laws which open up opportunities for citizens to serve in appointed government leadership posts and grassroots political party leadership roles. For this work, Harry received a Doctor of Humane Letters from Monmouth University.

In 1992, Harry led a bottom up reform fight and took over the chairmanship of what was then the most powerful political party organization in New Jersey, transferring the power over party endorsements to grassroots representatives. In 1995, Harry was elected to a county government position with executive and legislative power serving 750,000 residents. In this role, he authored and implemented a "Code of Conduct" requiring competitive hiring practices and competitive leasing contracts. To further ensure the integrity of government contracting on a statewide basis, Harry went on to lead the development and passage of what the New York Times reported was the strongest Pay-to-Play reform law in the nation.

Harry is a 1969 graduate of Brown University and holds a law degree from Fordham Law School. In 1973, he founded a law firm specializing in growth planning and environmental law. He co-authored an encyclopedia of Land Use Law in 1985 (West Publishing Co.) and served as chairman of the committee that developed and passed New Jersey's Fair Housing Act. He is also credited by former Governor Tom Kean for his leadership in developing and gaining passage of the State Planning Act.

Harry and his wife, Caroline, and their two daughters and sons-in-law, reside in Perth Amboy, New Jersey.

SERVICE • CIVILITY • PRAGMATISM

THE
CIVIC TRUSTEE
HANDBOOK

■ TABLE OF CONTENTS ■

■ **SECTIONONE** ■

DEFINITIONS

1. WHAT IS NO-BLAME?

This is both a process and a strategy adhered to by Civic Trustees in order to keep the focus on their solutions in Trust meetings, in public efforts to advance their solutions, and in all other public venues. It means no finger-pointing and acting in a respectful way.

2. WHAT IS EVIDENCE BASED?

Solutions are evidence based when they are based on policies with proven success in towns or cities of similar demographics. When solutions are success based, they avoid ideological conflict. Evidence based solutions do not invite debates about "my idea versus your idea." They are about facts and proof of what has worked. Solutions may be based on a combination of evidence based policies.

3. WHAT IS COST EFFECTIVE?

Cost effective means that implementation of the solution will, in short order, be budget neutral or, even better, will save money. If initial costs are involved or budget savings are not sufficient to pay the cost of the solutions, alternative funding sources must be obtained. For example, crowd funding, grants, or other outside fundraising resources may be pursued in order that the solution, if it has any start-up costs, is budget neutral. Another way to make a solution budget neutral is to find waste in the current budget and eliminate it to offset the new costs associated with the solution.

4. WHAT IS POWER CIVICS FOR HIGH SCHOOL?

Power Civics is a project-based 10-hour teaching tool that introduces high school students to the information and skills they need to be effective citizens and emerging leaders in their own community – to learn how to leave their city better than they found it. For interested students, it provides accessible entry level public service opportunities – ones that they can immediately seize without having to run for public office – ones that prepare them to participate in politics and government at the state and national level in the future. Power Civics is designed to fit into mandatory high school History/Social Studies courses.

5. WHAT IS POWER CIVICS FOR COLLEGE & ADULTS?

Power Civics combines the basic elements of the high school version with more advanced guidance on how to devise and successfully implement a solution to a city issue. Power Civics is available at many community colleges and universities and online for all. Please visit The Citizens Campaign website for complete information.

6. WHAT IS A NO-BLAME SOLUTIONS FORUM?

No-Blame Solutions Forums are community-based forums hosted by a Civic Trust exclusively for Civic Trustees (including potential recruits) and for local government decision makers who have the power to adopt or implement solutions in the issue area of the Solutions Forum. Decision makers may include elected and appointed officials, as well as town or school district administrators and employees and experts who might be involved in the adoption or implementation of a solution.

No-Blame Solutions Forums include a panel of experts on the subject issue, recruited from universities, professional associations and similar sources. Experts should be prepared to offer evidence based solutions that are cost effective and can be implemented locally. Importantly, all participants are invited to participate in a constructive dialogue with a No-Blame approach with the goal of identifying evidence based, cost effective solutions.

7. WHAT IS A BREAKOUT SESSION?

Breakout Sessions take place at Civic Trust meetings where members of each Issue Committee meet separately to discuss progress and steps taken to develop and advance a solution the Committee is working on. A Get Results Form is completed at the end of each Breakout Session.

8. WHAT IS A GET RESULTS FORM?

This is a form that lists the membership and attendance of the Issue Committee members and the commitments each member makes to develop and advance a Solution in preparation for the next solutions session meeting (see Sample in this Handbook).

9. WHAT IS A CIVIC TRUST ROSTER SHEET?

A Civic Trust Roster sheet tracks Civic Trustee attendance at Civic Trust meetings and the status of each one's No-Blame Problem Solving training (see Sample in this Handbook).

10. WHAT IS A RECAP MEMO?

A Recap Memo is a summary of the Civic Trust meeting that is sent to Civic Trustees after each meeting (See Sample in this Handbook).

11. WHAT IS A CIVIC TRUSTEE?

Civic Trustees are problem solvers who address issues in the community. They help public officials work with the No-Blame Problem Solving Process. They act as agents of empowerment as guest lecturers at community colleges, high school Power Civics classes and civic-minded community-based organizations.

12. WHAT IS A PROVISIONAL TRUSTEE?

A Provisional Trustee has submitted an application to become a Civic Trustee but the individual has not yet completed the required training. While they are Provisional Trustees, they cannot vote on matters that come before the Trust. Once the training is completed, however, they will receive a Certificate of Graduation and become full-fledged Civic Trustees with all the rights and responsibilities that come with that status (See Sample Certificate of Graduation in this Handbook).

13. WHAT IS A CIVIC TRUST ADMINISTRATOR?

A Civic Trust Administrator is a Civic Trustee chosen by the Trust that coordinates fellow Civic Trustees to attend monthly meetings via emails, phone calls or text messages. They assist with the setup of seating arrangements, the buffet table for food and, when required, they set up registration and panelist tables for Civic Trust No-Blame Solutions Forums. Should there be a budget available for food, Civic Trust Administrators would be responsible for ordering dinner and having it delivered to the Civic Trust meetings.

Other duties performed by a Civic Trust Administrator include collection of the Get Results Forms and the management of the Civic Trustee attendance roster, which tracks those who complete a year of service, and the 3-year term limit of Civic Trustees. Although it is the duty of all Civic Trustees to promote their own Civic Trust, Civic Trust Administrators also use social media recruitment strategies (see Recruitment Section in this Handbook) to promote Civic Trusteeship opportunities with their fellow citizens.

14. WHAT IS A CIVIC TRUST FACILITATOR?

Each Civic Trust should have at least two Civic Trust Facilitators to run the agenda and to help keep Civic Trustees focused on finding solutions in accordance with the step-by-step, No-Blame Problem Solving method. Having multiple Civic Trustees designated as Facilitators ensures that Civic Trusts can have effective meetings, even if one Facilitator is unavailable. Civic Trusts may have more than 2 Facilitators, but they must be chosen by a vote of the Civic Trust membership.

Civic Trust meetings are generally rich with information about your city and are structured to discuss issues that are chosen by Civic Trustees. Keeping Civic Trust issues on track with the No-Blame Problem Solving process, while also ensuring that enough time is allotted for Issue Committee Breakout Sessions at the meeting, are just a few of the duties performed by a Civic Trust Facilitator.

Other duties include running a results driven agenda, maintaining a No-Blame environment in Civic Trust meetings, and helping the Trust Administrator collect the Get Results Forms from Issue Committees (see Get Results Form in this Handbook). Information collected by the Civic Trust Facilitator may be placed on the following Civic Trust meeting agenda to keep Civic Trustees informed of their progress.

■ ■ ■

CIVIC TRUSTEES

Commitments, Qualifications, and Responsibilities

1. WHAT IS A CIVIC TRUSTEE?

Civic Trustees are problem solvers who address issues in the community. They help public officials work with the No-Blame Problem Solving Process. They act as agents of empowerment serving as guest lecturers at community colleges, high school Power Civics classes and civic-minded community-based organizations.

2. WHAT ARE THE COMMITMENTS OF A CIVIC TRUSTEE?

A Civic Trustee commits to participate in monthly meetings called "Solutions Sessions" for a minimum of one year (except for August and December) where they work with fellow Trustees to address issues they prioritize, using the 10 Step "No-Blame Problem Solving" process. They are excused up to 3 absences, but Civic Trustees who miss more than 3 meetings would not be invited back to the Civic Trust.

3. WHAT ARE THE PREREQUISITES FOR BECOMING AND SERVING AS A CIVIC TRUSTEE?

A. Trustees must complete a Civic Trustee application;

B. Trustees must take the "No-Blame Problem Solving" training found in online Power Civics (each video is approximately 6 minutes long);

C. Trustees must be at least 18 years old, however Junior Civic Trustees may qualify to serve at 16 years of age with the consent of a parent or guardian;

D. Trustees may not be an elected official or chairperson of a political party or campaign committee or a candidate for elected office. Spokespersons or chiefs of staff for these individuals are also prohibited from becoming Trustees.

Furthermore, an existing Civic Trustee who announces his or her candidacy for any of the above described offices, must immediately resign their Trusteeship. However, participation in political parties or serving on a government board or commission is not a disqualifier.

These above qualifications are intended to preserve the citizen driven agenda of Civic Trustees as described in the Civic Pledge.

E. Civic Trustees must abide by the Civic Pledge and its No-Blame requirement at all times and in all circumstances during their term of service.

THE CIVIC PLEDGE

I pledge to leave my community and country better than I found them by pursuing practical solutions instead of just pointing out problems and assigning blame.

NOTE: All Civic Trustees who have served for a year or more shall be recognized by a Resolution of Service issued by The Citizens Campaign and shall be entitled to all the benefits of participation in the Civic Trust Community (See Sample Resolution of Service in this Handbook).

4. WHAT DEFINES THE "PRACTICAL SOLUTIONS" COMMITTED TO BY TRUSTEES IN THE CIVIC PLEDGE?

Practical Solutions are those that are cost effective and based on policies with proven success. They are practical because when cost effective, i.e. budget neutral and evidence based, they avoid the ideological conflicts that so often preclude progress.

5. WHAT ARE THE RESPONSIBILITIES OF A CIVIC TRUSTEE?

Civic Trustees:

A. commit to serve a term of one year and are disqualified if they miss more than three of the monthly Solutions Sessions;

B. may not serve for more than three consecutive years, but after their three years of service, may participate in non-voting matters in all Civic Trust meetings and other activities, as long as they abide by the "No-Blame" provision of the Civic Pledge;

C. find practical solutions and adapt them for adoption in their own communities using the 10-Step No-Blame Problem Solving Guide;

D. host No-Blame Solutions Forums on issues of importance for decision makers in their communities;

E. promote civic empowerment by seeking the adoption of Power Civics in their town's high schools or community colleges;

F. serve as guest speakers in high school and college Power Civics classes and Power Civics Community Forums;

G. recruit new Trustees;

H. respond accordingly to Civic Trust communications including emails, texts, and phone calls.

■ **SECTIONTHREE** ■
CIVIC TRUSTS

1. WHAT IS A CIVIC TRUST?

Civic Trusts are non-partisan, unincorporated associations of Civic Trustees. It is highly recommended that there be at least 12 Trustees in a Civic Trust of a town of less than 50,000 and 24 Trustees in a city of 50,000 or more. These minimums make it possible for Civic Trusts to work on multiple issues at a time and ensure a constant stream of solutions. Civic Trusts are flat organizations in that they have no chairpersons.

2. WHAT ROLES OF TRUSTEES KEEP CIVIC TRUSTS VITAL?

Ideally, Civic Trusts should select one or more members of the Trust for each of the following role(s) and tasks:

A. Civic Trust Administrator

B. Civic Trust Facilitators

C. Lead recruitment drives to enlist new Trustees

D. Serve as guest speakers in Power Civics classes and community forums

E. Lead organizing efforts to host No-Blame Solutions Forums

3. HOW DO CIVIC TRUSTS SELECT THE ISSUES THEY WILL ADDRESS?

A Civic Trustee may raise an issue they wish to address at any monthly Solutions Session when topics of new issues are being discussed on the agenda. The issue will move forward if at least three Trustees commit to work on it at the meeting. However, an Issue Committee of the Trust shall not be formed around the issue unless there are six Trustees who commit to serve on the committee by the next monthly Solutions Session. (Issue Committees require 6 people minimum per Committee, however, only 3 Trustees per Committee are required in cities of less than 50,000).

These minimum numbers insure that there are sufficient Trustees to research, develop, present and pursue a solution and so that Issue Committees incorporate a variety of skill sets and have the ability to proceed if a committee member withdraws or cannot proceed due to illness or personal circumstances.

4. WHEN CAN A SOLUTION BE PRESENTED FOR ADOPTION BY ANY GIVEN CIVIC TRUST?

Solutions must be evidence based, cost effective and beneficial to the community as a whole. They must also be able to be adopted at the local level; this includes the municipal, school district or county level. Also, a Solution must have the affirmative vote of the majority of the Civic Trustees at a meeting with a quorum of Civic Trustees before it can be publically and formally presented as a Solution of the Civic Trust.

ADDITIONAL INFORMATION ABOUT CIVIC TRUSTS

1. WHAT IS THE RELATIONSHIP OF A LOCAL CIVIC TRUST TO THE CITIZENS CAMPAIGN?

The Citizens Campaign assists local Trusts with the expert support of its Law & Policy Task Force after the local Trust provides a memo with the contents set forth in Step 7 of the No-Blame Problem Solving process. The National Civic Trust offers all the benefits to Trustees of the Civic Trust community, including invitations to Citizens Campaign events, new empowerment tools, camaraderie of fellow Trustees across the country and the mutual support they provide to each other.

2. THE CITIZENS CAMPAIGN MAY CEASE ITS SUPPORT AND RECOGNITION OF A LOCAL CIVIC TRUST:

A. When the number of Civics Trustees of the local Trust is fewer than the prescribed number or the regular attendance is less than 75% of the total Trust membership, it may cease to be recognized by The Citizens Campaign.

B. When one or more local Civic Trustees engages in personal attacks on public officials, they may be removed by a vote of their fellow Trustees after appropriate notice to cease. Remember: It is ok to debate policies, but there should be no personal attacks on the person or criticism of people's motives.

C. If a local Trust has multiple incidents of blame, it will cease to be recognized and supported by The Citizens Campaign.

D. If a Trust operates outside the parameters set forth in this Handbook without authorization from The Citizens Campaign's home office's Civic Trust Program Director, it may cease to be recognized by The Citizens Campaign.

3. THE COSTS FOR OPERATING A CIVIC TRUST:

Costs are usually low or non-existent, especially when Civic Trustees provide potluck meals for Trust meetings and meeting facilities are free. However, if there are costs that cannot be avoided, contact the home office of The Citizens Campaign for advice and/or support.

■ ■ ■

■ **SECTIONFOUR** ■

CREATING A CIVIC TRUST

This chapter highlights the necessary components for creation of a well-organized Civic Trust. It describes essential Civic Trustee roles and "issue" committees that keep Civic Trust solutions moving forward. This section also provides guidance for securing an ideal monthly meeting space, achieving required Civic Trustee membership thresholds, and for finding additional information about meeting costs, expert support, Help Desk assistance and more.

If you are interested in creating a local Trust, the first step you must take is to contact The Citizens Campaign's home office via email and indicate your interest in organizing a Civic Trust in your community. You will receive guidance on time saving steps for beginning the process of organizing a Trust and prerequisites for full support and recognition by The Citizens Campaign.

Secure a Monthly Meeting Place, Preferably at a Community College in Your Area:

One of the first things you want to do to create a Civic Trust is secure a convenient place to host monthly Civic Trust meetings (Solutions Sessions). Examples include community colleges, community schools or local libraries. These organizations have been known to partner with Civic Trust groups and have also served as valuable sources for the recruitment of potential Trustees. Community colleges are the best hosts as they are open in the evenings, usually have good parking, and can provide opportunities for learning Power Civics in both regular course offerings and adult education classes, thus providing a continuing training and recruitment complement to the needs of every Civic Trust.

The Citizens Campaign has a working relationship with many community colleges across the country, and your first step should be to contact The Citizens Campaign to ascertain if there is a community college in your area with which The Citizens Campaign has a relationship.

An ideal Civic Trust location will:

(1) accommodate all Trust members and guests around an arrangement of a square or rectangular tables;

(2) permit food to be delivered and eaten on premises;

(3) have good parking availability; and

(4) have audiovisual equipment to show videos for training and other purposes (This element is not critical if a laptop and screen or appropriate wall space is available).

No matter what location you secure, you will need to fill out an application form for the use of space. Be sure to include all your planned Civic Trust meeting dates to secure space for the entire year. Schedule your first meeting on a date and time convenient for prospective Civic Trustees to attend, and then confirm a firm date and time for each month thereafter (example: the 3rd Tuesday of each month at 6:00 p.m.).

If there is a charge for the use of space, or liability insurance is required, try another location. You may also consider hosting introductory sessions, i.e., Civic Trust Info Sessions, in your home until other members have joined and can help you with the official Civic Trust formation, including locating a meeting place.

Recruit at Least Half of the Trust Membership:

A qualifying Civic Trust in a city of 50,000 people or more requires a minimum of 24 Civic Trustees. A town with less than 50,000 residents requires a minimum of 12 trustees. When beginning to form a Civic Trust in a town with less than 50,000 people, start with a core group of 6 Civic Trustees. The core 6 will assist you with recruiting the other 6 needed to form a Civic Trust. If your city has more the 50,000 residents, start with a core of 12 Civic Trustees to assist with recruiting other members and to begin work on Trust building activities.

It is important to follow the steps in the Section dedicated to Recruitment in this Handbook. It contains useful information about building, maintaining and expanding Trust membership. Most importantly, it includes proven steps for recruitment.

You can also use the **"Model Memo for Potential Civic Trustee Recruits"** (Sample found in this Handbook) as a helpful tool in creating and building a Civic Trust in your community.

After you have identified a location for Trust meetings and the minimum number of members (6 in a town of less than 50,000 and 12 in a city of 50,000 or more) to create a Civic Trust, you should notify The Citizens Campaign's home office and you can start planning for the initial meeting of the Trust.

(A) WRITE TO THE CITIZENS CAMPAIGN'S HELP DESK

Once you have assembled the threshold elements for building a Civic Trust, it's time to once again contact The Citizens Campaign's Help Desk. Write to helpdesk@thecitizenscampaign.org and tell us:

(1) where the first meeting will take place;

(2) the names of Trustee applicants and links to their applications;

(3) who will be serving as the Civic Trust Administrator (see below);

(4) who will be serving as the initial two Facilitators (see below);

(5) if there are any cost issues;

(6) the best time to contact you to provide guidance with next steps.

Identify a Civic Trust Administrator:

A Civic Trust Administrator is a Civic Trustee chosen by the Trust who coordinates fellow Civic Trustees to attend monthly meetings via emails, phone calls or text messages. They assist with the setup of seating arrangements, the buffet table for food and, when required, they set up registration and panelist tables for Civic Trust No-Blame Solutions Forums. Should there be a budget available for food, Civic Trust Administrators would be responsible for ordering dinner and having it delivered to the Civic Trust meetings.

Other duties performed by a Civic Trust Administrator include collection of the Get Results Forms and the management of the Civic Trustee attendance roster, which tracks those who complete a year of service and the 3-year term limit of Civic Trustees. Although it is the duty of all Civic Trustees to promote their own Civic Trust, Civic Trust Administrators also use social media recruitment strategies (see Recruitment Section in this Handbook) to promote Civic Trusteeship opportunities to their fellow citizens.

Identify Two Civic Trust Facilitators:

Each Civic Trust should have at least two Civic Trust Facilitators to run the agenda and to help keep Civic Trustees focused on finding solutions in accordance with the step-by-step, No-Blame Problem Solving method. Having multiple Civic Trustees designated as Facilitators ensures that Civic Trusts can have effective meetings even if one Facilitator is unavailable. Civic Trusts may have more than 2 Facilitators, but they must be chosen by a vote of the Civic Trust membership.

Civic Trust meetings are generally rich with information about your city and are structured to discuss issues that are chosen by Civic Trustees. Keeping Civic Trust issues on track with the No-Blame Problem Solving process, while also ensuring that enough time is allotted for Issue Committee Breakout Sessions at the meeting, are just a few of the duties performed by a Civic Trust Facilitator.

Other duties include running a results driven agenda, maintaining a No-Blame environment in Civic Trust meetings, and helping the Trust Administrator collect the Get Results Forms from Issue Committees (see Get Results Form in this Handbook). Information collected by the Civic Trust Facilitator may be placed on the following Civic Trust meeting agenda to keep Civic Trustees informed of their progress.

(B) At the first meeting, time should be set aside for the Trust members, as a group, to watch the video Part 1 – The No-Blame Problem Solving Process and review the Solutions Sharing Platform on The Citizens Campaign website.

(C) A laptop should be available at the meeting so that Civic Trustee applications can be completed and submitted.

(D) Follow the steps outlined in the Section on Preparing for a Civic Trust Meeting in this Handbook.

■   ■   ■

PREPARING FOR A CIVIC TRUST MEETING

This chapter provides information about preparing for the first meeting of a Civic Trust and a step-by-step guide for preparing for all Civic Trust meetings.

Preparing for the initial organizing meeting of a local Civic Trust:

After you have assembled the threshold elements for building a Civic Trust, you should start planning for the first meeting of the Civic Trust.

(A) Identify a Civic Trust Administrator:

A Civic Trust Administrator is a Civic Trustee chosen by the Trust that coordinates fellow Civic Trustees to attend monthly meetings via emails, phone calls or text messages. They assist with the setup of seating arrangements, the buffet table for food and, when required, they set up registration and panelist tables for Civic Trust No-Blame Solutions Forums. Should there be a budget available for food, Civic Trust Administrators would be responsible for ordering dinner and having it delivered to the Civic Trust meetings.

Other duties performed by a Civic Trust Administrator include collection of the Get Results Forms and the management of the Civic Trustee attendance roster, which tracks those who complete a year of service, and the 3-year term limit of Civic Trustees. Although it is the duty of all Civic Trustees to promote their own Civic Trust, Civic Trust Administrators also use social media recruitment strategies (see Recruitment Section in this Handbook) to promote Civic Trusteeship opportunities with their fellow citizens.

(B) Identify two Civic Trust Facilitators:

Each Civic Trust should have at least two Civic Trust Facilitators to run the agenda and to help keep Civic Trustees focused on finding solutions in accordance with the step-by-step, No-Blame Problem Solving method. Having multiple Civic Trustees designated as Facilitators ensures that Civic Trusts can have effective meetings, even if one Facilitator is unavailable. Civic Trusts may have more than 2 Facilitators, but they must be chosen by a vote of the Civic Trust membership.

Civic Trust meetings are generally rich with information about your city and are structured to discuss issues that are chosen by Civic Trustees. Keeping Civic Trust issues on track with the No-Blame Problem Solving process, while also ensuring that enough time is allotted for Issue Committee Breakout Sessions at the meeting, are just a few of the duties performed by a Civic Trust Facilitator.

Other duties include running a results driven agenda, maintaining a No-Blame environment in Civic Trust meetings, and helping the Trust Administrator collect the Get Results Forms from Issue Committees (see Get Results Form in this Handbook). Information collected by the Civic Trust Facilitator may be placed on the following Civic Trust meeting agenda to keep Civic Trustees informed of their progress.

(C)WRITE TO THE CITIZENS CAMPAIGN'S HELP DESK

Once you have assembled the threshold elements for building a Civic Trust, it's time to once again contact The Citizens Campaign's Help Desk. Write to helpdesk@thecitizenscampaign.org and tell us:

(1) where the Trust meetings will take place;

(2) the names of Trustee applicants and links to their applications;

(3) who will be serving as the Civic Trust Administrator;

(4) who will be serving as the initial two Facilitators;

(5) any cost issues;

(6) the best time to contact you to provide guidance with next steps.

At the first meeting, time should be set aside for the Trust members, as a group, to watch the video *Part 1 – The No-Blame Problem Solving Process* and review the Solutions Sharing Platform on The Citizens Campaign website.

A laptop should be available at the meeting so that new Civic Trustee applications can be completed and submitted.

Follow the steps outlined in this Section for preparing for regular Civic Trust meetings.

How Civic Trust Administrators Prepare for Civic Trust Solutions Sessions (monthly meetings):

Prepare an Agenda:

Begin drafting an agenda the day after each meeting and include the following items:

1. An agenda should include a title at the top of the page in the center

2. Date, time, and location of the meeting on the left hand side

3. Next meeting date and location on the right-hand side

4. Each agenda line should be numbered and indicate a beginning and ending time

5. Dinner and fellowship is always item #1 on the agenda

6. Introduction of members and guests is item #2

7. Include motivational stories and reports of significant progress

8. Identify any guest speakers and include a Q&A session following any presentation

9. New issue discussion proposals (discussion of new issues should not begin until at least 3 Trustees volunteer to work on the issue)

10. Breakout sessions

11. Closing remarks & adjournment

Sample Timeframe for a Solutions Session:

A. 6:00 pm–Dinner and Welcome of guests and new Trustees, with existing Trustees and prospective Trustees introducing themselves and stating what motivates them to participate, if they wish.

B. 6:30 pm–Progress Reports by Issue Committees and requests for new issues.

C. 7:00 pm–Breakout session for Issues Committees to work on their respective solutions and completion of Get Results Forms.

D. 8:00 pm–Closing Remarks & Adjournment including any clean-up.

Communicate with Civic Trustees, potential Trustees, Guests and all other expected attendees with information about the meetings including the following:

1. **Potential Civic Trustees:** On the day after a Civic Trust meeting, invite potential new Civic Trustees, who submitted a Civic Trust application, to the following month's meeting by phone or email. When you actively engage potential Civic Trustees the next day, they feel welcomed, and are more likely to become committed participants at the Civic Trust meetings. If there were guests that attended the previous Civic Trust meeting, but have not submitted an application, contact them to see if they are interested in becoming Civic Trustees and

inform them that guests are only allowed to attend one meeting. Should they wish to continue participating in monthly Solutions Sessions, they must apply to become Civic Trustees. Use the "Memo for Potential Civic Trustee Recruits" (see Sample in this Handbook), to help candidates understand the requirements and benefits of becoming Civic Trustees.

2. **Civic Trustees:** Send Civic Trustees meeting reminders. Three reminders are suggested:

   (1) An update memo reviewing progress made or reported at the last meeting and a request for RSVPs;

   (2) A draft agenda with request for input and a second RSVP request;

   (3) A final RSVP request.

   With everything moving so fast in the 21st century, it's easy to forget what we have scheduled on our calendars, but if you send out frequent reminders, Civic Trustees will have the meeting date fresh on their minds. To help ensure a good attendance, it is recommended that you email, call and text reminders in between Civic Trust meetings.

3. **Guest Speakers, Experts, and Professionals:** Confirm any guest speakers, if necessary. There are times that guest speakers are invited to present to the Civic Trust when they are knowledgeable in the issue areas that Civic Trustees are working on, especially when a No-Blame Solutions Forum is being coordinated. Whenever guest speakers are invited to present, be sure to follow up a month in advance and a few days before the meeting to confirm their attendance.

4. **Outreach for the Civic Trust meeting:** On an ongoing basis, post the Civic Trust meeting on social media and in local media outlets. Use the ideas and suggestions found in the Recruitment Section of this Handbook to invite potential Trustees to the meeting. Send a press release to local media outlets when Civic Trustees have success with their solutions and also when they are planning to host a No-Blame Solutions Forum with expert panelists (Please review the Recruitment Section in this Handbook for information and sample materials regarding outreach for new Civic Trustees).

5. **Prior to each meeting, update the Civic Trust Roster Sheet** (See sample Civic Trust Roster Sheet in this Handbook) with the following information:

   • Keep track of Civic Trustee attendance to ensure Trustees have not missed more than the maximum times allowed; three unexcused absences will result in disqualification. The three absences do not include the months of August and December, when meetings are not scheduled.

   • Track who has completed the No-Blame Problem Solving Training (the requirement to become a Trustee is to submit an application after the initial visit. The individual then becomes a "Provisional Trustee" until completion of the next scheduled No-Blame Problem Solving Training, after which they will receive a Certificate of Graduation (See the sample Certificate of Graduation in this Handbook).

6. **Call Civic Trustees who missed the meetings.** If there is no reason for the absence, remind the Trustee of the attendance policy.

7. **Add recent guest contact information to the database** (these guests are potential Trustees). Remember, there must be 12 to 24 members to maintain a Civic Trust.

   A. Follow up with a call to guests who attended the Civic Trust meeting and:

      • Ask if they are interested in becoming a Civic Trustee

      • If yes, review the Model Memo for Potential Civic Trustee Recruits (Sample is in this Handbook)

      • Ask if they will take the No-Blame Civic Pledge

      • Ask them to complete and submit an application

8. **Call Issue Committee members during the interval between meetings** to find out the status of their "action steps" and to see if they need help or advice.

Other Advance Preparations:

9. **Confirm the availability of the facility** or location of the meeting, if necessary. Depending on the location of the Civic Trust meetings, you may be required to submit forms on a monthly basis to secure space. Be sure to submit appropriate

forms in a timely manner to secure Civic Trust meeting space in advance.

10. **Follow up with the Civic Trust Facilitator**. Since Civic Trusts have multiple Facilitators, make sure you have confirmed the Trustee who will be facilitating the next meeting. Facilitators should be made aware of any new guests that may have RSVP'd their attendance to the Civic Trust Administrator.

11. **Prepare Civic Trust Meeting Handouts**. Below is a list of handouts that the Administrator should print in advance for Civic Trust meetings:

   A. Sign in Sheet (See Sample in this Handbook)

   B. Civic Trust Agenda (See Sample in this Handbook)

   C. General Civic Trust Application (See Sample in this Handbook)

   D. Junior Civic Trustee Application (See Sample in this Handbook)

   E. Civic Trustee Handbook

   F. Civic Pledge (See Sample in this Handbook)

   G. 10 Step No-Blame Problem Solving Guide

   H. Get Results Form (See Sample in this Handbook)

   I. Civic Trust Roster Sheet (See Sample in this Handbook)

   J. Voter Registration Forms

   K. Articles related to issues being worked on by Civic Trustees (Optional)

   In addition to handouts, think through anything that you might need to keep the meeting running smoothly. Discuss the Agenda with the Facilitator to see if you will need additional handouts for the Civic Trust meeting. Other items you may consider bringing include, but are not limited to, pens, pencils, markers, poster boards, note pads and the like.

12. **Order dinner for the Civic Trust.** If your Civic Trust has a budget for ordering dinner, we recommend that you offer protein, carbs, and vegetables. Civic Trustees usually come straight from work or school when they attend Civic Trust meetings, and typically come hungry. A full meal helps Civic

Trustees feel well-nourished and energized to do No-Blame Problem Solving in their cities. Feel free to vary food options, but ask for feedback from Civic Trustees. A general food order may consist of roasted chicken, mashed potatoes, vegetables, and bottled water. To help with serving the food, have serving and eating utensils ready for use at each meeting. Lastly, save time by having the food delivered 15 minutes before the meeting.

13. **Arrive early to prep Civic Trust Meeting Room Space**. Set up tables in a conference style fashion (a square or rectangle) so that everyone is seeing each other during the meeting. Reserve the front and center seat for the facilitator who runs the agenda. If food has been ordered, set up a buffet table for when it arrives. You may also need to set up audio and visual equipment for a presentation.

14. **A laptop should be available at all meetings so that new Civic Trustee applications can be completed and submitted.**

■ ■ ■

■ **SECTIONSIX** ■

FACILITATING A CIVIC TRUST MEETING

This chapter outlines steps that should be taken when facilitating a Civic Trust meeting.

- **Pass around the sign in sheet** that includes the name, phone and email contact information for all attendees and ask if everyone will please sign in. This is important information to keep track of (See Sample in this Handbook).

- **The Facilitator convenes the meeting** by welcoming Civic Trustees and guests and briefly states the basic tenets of the Civic Trust's focus on solutions in a No-Blame environment developed using a proven 10-Step process. Civic Trustees and guests should be invited to make a 30 second introduction of who they are and why they joined the Civic Trust, if they so wish.

  - **Facilitator duties**: Follow the agenda step-by-step. Overall time management is important: prevent too much off-agenda chatter and stay on point. Issues discussed should occur in breakout sessions except for brief progress reports and introduction of potential new issues. This is to avoid anyone monopolizing meeting time and to preserve time for issue Breakout Sessions.

  - **The Facilitator will give a home office report** (on, for example, upcoming events, new Civic Cities, nationwide progress and recent solutions successes by other Trusts).

  - **Continue to move through the Agenda** as scheduled (there may be exceptions such as requests for clarity, questions, confirmations, etc.).
    - Keep Civic Trustees on track with respect to the Agenda by reminding Trustees about the importance of covering all topics on the Agenda, and maintaining the focus on solutions and practicing No-Blame.

- **When you reach the Agenda item, "New Issues"**, the Trustees may form Issue Committees: (6 people minimum per Committee; 3 per Committee in cities of less than 50,000). Each committee should be named for the specific issue to be addressed and individuals must be willing to serve on that committee until a solution is achieved. Each committee chooses a Breakout Coordinator for the meeting's breakout sessions.

- **Breakout sessions**: Facilitators should help with the duties of the Issue Committee's Breakout Coordinator:

  (a) He/she will begin by filling out the top portion of the Get Results Form including point number 1 (See Sample in this Handbook);

  (b) Identify which step the Issue Committee is on by using the No-Blame Problem Solving Guide;

  (c) Discuss doable steps that can be taken by Civic Trustees, and list them on point number 2 of the Get Results Form.

- Allow approximately 30 minutes for issues to be worked through using the 10-Step, No-Blame guide (you won't cover all 10 steps in one meeting, but try to cover steps 1 through 3 in the first meeting).

- **The Breakout Coordinator reports back** to the Facilitators and the full Trust membership to share the plan of action along with the Get Results Form's action steps. The Get Results Form will indicate the assigned tasks for each committee member. The Form should be turned over to the Administrator and he/she will scan a copy of the Form back to the Breakout Coordinator the day after the meeting, and follow up on action steps progress later in the month prior to the next meeting.

- **The Facilitator offers closing remarks**, thanking Trustees and guests for attending the meeting; also asks guests to apply to become Civic Trustees and reminding them that they can only attend the Civic Trust meeting one time as guests (It is advisable to have a laptop available at meetings so that new Civic Trustee applications can be completed and submitted at the meeting).

- **The Facilitator spearheads clean up** asking Civic Trustees to help put the meeting space back to its original condition and encouraging them to take home any leftover food.

- **Everyone exits** the building with the Facilitator making sure to close windows, turn out lights, etc.

■ ■ ■

■ **SECTIONSEVEN** ■

RECRUITMENT

For a Civic Trust to thrive, recruitment of new Trustees needs to be a constant major focus and current Trustees must all be enlisted as recruiters. This is not only the case when a Trust is initially being formed; it is critical at all times for infusions of new energy and new ideas as Trusts mature.

This chapter provides a hands-on guide to recruitment for people seeking to form a Civic Trust and to add new Trustees to an existing one. It covers recruitment by current Civic Trustees, recruiting from civic-minded organizations, prime recruitment windows, the use of social media, and recruitment at community colleges where Trust meetings are often hosted.

Engaging Civic Trustees in Recruitment:

Civic Trustees and former Civic Trustees are always your best recruiters, whether they are the initial group of Trustees working to create the Trust or they have served as long-time Civic Trustees in a well-established Civic Trust. They can speak genuinely with family, friends, neighbors and fellow city residents about why they have decided to be a Trustee and, once they gain experience in a Trust, share why they find it meaningful, the high quality training they have received and how the Civic Trust is working effectively to make improvements in their City. This approach of recruiting via personal outreach is the most effective, especially when Civic Trustees are passionate about their work.

The following are materials Civic Trustees will need when recruiting either one-on-one, at events, or when making presentations to organizations.

1. A Civic Trust Meeting Flyer (see Sample Civic Trust Meeting Flyer in this Handbook): Possible design elements on the Flyer could include, but certainly are not limited to:

    A. Catchy questions or statements. Here are some examples:

    1. Be a part of the decision-making process in your city!

    2. You have more power than you think you have!

    3. Want to learn how to become a city problem solver?

    4. Learn techniques used by successful practitioners that transform city issues into solutions!

    B. Designs or images that show Problem Solving or Civic Trustees working on issues

C. Essential Information; the benefits of becoming a Civic Trustee; location of Civic Trust meetings; and date and time of the meetings.

2.   Civic Trustee Application - Available on The Citizens Campaign website for both print and download (see Sample in this Handbook.

3.   Model Memo for Potential Civic Trustee Recruits (see Sample in this Handbook).

Targeting Civic-Minded Organizations:

One-on-one outreach should be supplemented by recruitment pitches and presentations at meetings of civic-minded organizations. Pitches can be done by the Civic Trust organizer or experienced Trust members. Trusts can set up a Speakers Task Force to line up these speaking engagements and send out speakers. Showing one of the videos available on The Citizens Campaign website can enhance the pitch, along with the marketing materials. Top Targets include:

- Community College civic and student government organizations
- Churches in economically challenged neighborhoods
- Service clubs
- Parent/Teacher Organizations
- Veterans organizations
- Local Non-profits

It is important to let community non-profits know that the Civic Trust provides leadership training. Civic Trustees don't compete with local non-profits because they don't hold permanent positions and they are term-limited after 3 years of service.

Prime Recruitment Windows:

While recruitment is a year-round activity, the two recommended annual recruitment windows are August 15th–September 15th and January 15th–February 15th. These windows are timed for the beginning of Fall and Spring semesters at community and other colleges, along with other benefits, such as taking advantage of the fact that many people are more likely to make new commitments at the beginning of the year.   This is the best time for intensive recruitment campaigns and motivating existing Civic Trustees to do stepped-up one-on-one recruiting. **Setting a goal for each Trustee of bringing one new recruit to the September and February Trust meetings is one tested way of bringing in a sufficient number of new recruits.**

At the beginning of recruitment periods, a media release should be sent out to local news outlets as well as posted on social media (see Sample Media Release in this Handbook). Sending out another release a week before the close of the window or application period is often effective as well.

Effectively Using Social Media:

Social Media is a tested and useful tool for recruiting Civic Trustees. To maximize exposure, it's good to have 3 rotating campaigns for each social media website listed below. Each campaign posted should ask the audience to interact by applying to become a Civic Trustee, signing up for a No-Blame Problem Solving training, and reposting and hash-tagging. Following are the social media websites that work best for this purpose with sample recruitment campaigns:

Facebook

Here is an example of a 3 week cycle with posting every other day. It fits well within the prime recruiting windows. Boosting these posts will provide much greater reach and yield better results.

1. Media: Newark, the Civic City Video (https://youtu.be/W4onxC5tNgo); Messaging: Do you want to make your City the next "Civic City", click on the link below to register for the next Civic Trust meeting. A lite dinner will be served, but you need to register for the Trust meeting.

2. Media: Image of the book, Citizen Power (https://thecitizenscampaign.org/power-civics/citizenpower/); Messaging: Turn your political frustrations into solutions. This book teaches citizens techniques used by practitioners of local government that transformed cities using proven policies. To find out how to get your free copy of the book, visit www.thecitizenscampaign.org.

3. Media: Newark, the Civic City Video (https://youtu.be/W4onxC5tNgo); Messaging: Jr. Civic Trustee Bradley Gonmiah exercised his citizen rights and presented a solution that empowers all students in Newark to become City Problem Solvers. His solution was adopted unanimously. To learn the techniques he used to implement his solution, join a Civic Trust!

To improve advertisement results, inbox every person who engages with the Facebook post. For example, if someone likes or comments on the post, inbox them with a thank you, and invite the individual to the next Civic Trust meeting. This personalizes the engagement and opens up opportunities for the Facebook user to ask more questions. For efficiency, copy and paste the same thank you response for each Facebook user when you engage. Additionally, enlist Civic Trustees to share and like the Facebook posts. This will generate a viral effect.

You may also choose to target public Facebook groups that exist in your city. You may be required to become a member of the group prior to posting, which you can do easily on the Facebook group page. These groups help identify citizens who are active in the community without having to physically meet them. If you're not sure what Facebook group pages exist in your city, type the city name in the search box. If there are any groups created in Facebook, they will show up in the search feed. Do not overpost in the group pages. Doing so could have you removed by the group administrator(s).

Paid Facebook advertisements are also helpful with getting information out to targeted groups. You can hyper focus on groups that include individuals such as educators, veterans, and students, to name a few. When you purchase advertisement through Facebook, you can also select specific areas such as a city, county, or state, and choose the times the posts are made. To ensure that money is not being wasted, start off with a small amount to see if your post produces the results you're looking for. If it does, consider investing a larger amount of money into the campaign ad for greater exposure. Unless you have experience in this area, we recommend contacting the Help Desk if you would like to do an advertising campaign.

Instagram

Here is an example of a recruitment campaign that can be posted in a 3 week cycle every other day on Instagram.

1. Image: Citizens at the ballot box (Google search an image); Message: Civic engagement can be more than just voting; Link Button: Learn More A. The link button should take the user to the Civic Trust page to apply

2. Image: You Have More Power than Think You Have! Message: Click the link to get a free copy of the guide that helped citizens implement over 300 local laws; Link Button: Get the No-Blame Problem Solving Guide B. The link button should direct users to the 10 Step No-Blame Problem Solving Guide on The Citizens Campaign's website.

3. Video: Introduction to Power Civics video (https://youtu.be/ FTwSfl4LVcA). Message: This is how we fill in the 40 year gap of Civics not being taught in schools; Link Button: Learn more C. The link button should direct users to the Power Civics Online page.

Just like Facebook, you can increase your advertisement results by engaging with Instagram followers that like your post. Instagram is typically not used to recruit members into organizations, but it still can engage people and peak their interest!

Recruiting at Community Colleges:

Community Colleges mainly attract students and adults who live in and stay in the cities, towns, and counties in which they are located. That makes them excellent recruiting locations. In several cities, The Civic Trust is hosted by the local community college and the college is teaching Power Civics as a component of political science or other related subject area courses.

Listed below are tips for recruiting Trustees at community colleges. These tips apply to colleges and universities across the board:

- Identify Community College publications and contact the College Communications Director to request inclusion of information in these publications about how to apply to be a Civic Trustee.

- If there is a student newspaper, contact the editor and ask to submit an article or ask the paper to cover a Civic Trust meeting.

- Ask whether a message about the Civic Trust and how to apply can be sent out to all students via email.

- Ensure that all professors teaching Power Civics as a component of their course are given specific information about the Civic Trust for their students.

- Contact the Chair of the Political Science Department and any other Department where Power Civics is being taught and ask whether a note about the Civic Trust can be included in any Department Communication with students.

- Identify and target Civic-oriented clubs and service organizations, including fraternities and sororities.

- Identify and target student government and civic engagement organizations and similar extracurricular activity groups.

Obtain a schedule of information days most colleges hold for students to learn about campus and community organizations. These usually take place early in the semester or during orientation. Request permission to set up a Civic Trust table/information booth. If only formal campus organizations are permitted to table, go to the event and talk to the targeted organizations about scheduling a presentation/pitch.

▪ ▪ ▪

■ **SECTIONEIGHT** ■

SAMPLE FORMS

SAMPLE: GET RESULTS FORM

Trustee Reporting: _____   Date: _____

Issue Committee Name: _____

   1. Issue Committee Members and Attendance

Members: Attendance:

(Please print names)   (Please check box for members in attendance)

_____ ☐   _____ ☐

_____ ☐   _____ ☐

_____ ☐   _____ ☐

Priorities (List solutions being pursued in priority order)

      A. _____

      B. _____

      C. _____

   2. List action to be taken before next Trust meeting and the Trustees agreeing to take the
      specified actions; (examples include specific research assignments or government records
      request; meeting(s) with public officials; contacting The Citizens Campaign, etc.)

Specific Action   Person Responsible   Step for Action
                                               (In the No-Blame Problem Solving Guide)

  1. _____

  2. _____

  3. _____

SAMPLE: ROSTER SHEET

Active Trustees			Trained on 10 Step?	Meetings Attended										Total Meetings Attended
Last Name	First Name	Start Date	Received 10 Step Training?	1/16/2019	2/20/2019	3/20/2019	4/17/2019	5/15/2019	6/19/2019	7/17/2019	9/18/2019	10/16/2019	11/20/2019	
insert Civic Trustee name	insert Civic Trustee name	1/16/2019	Yes	1	1	1	1	1		1	1		1	8
insert Civic Trustee name	insert Civic Trustee name	1/16/2019	Yes	1	1						1	1		4
insert Civic Trustee name	insert Civic Trustee name	1/16/2019	Yes	1	1	1		1	1			1		6
insert Civic Trustee name	insert Civic Trustee name	1/16/2019	Yes	1	1			1		1				4
insert Civic Trustee name	insert Civic Trustee name	1/16/2019	Yes	1		1		1					1	4
insert Civic Trustee name	insert Civic Trustee name	1/16/2019	Yes	1	1		1	1	1	1	1	1	1	8
insert Civic Trustee name	insert Civic Trustee name	1/16/2019	Yes	1	1	1	1	1	1	1	1	1	1	8
insert Civic Trustee name	insert Civic Trustee name	1/16/2019	Yes	1		1	1	1		1			1	5
insert Civic Trustee name	insert Civic Trustee name	1/16/2019	Yes	1		1							1	3
insert Civic Trustee name	insert Civic Trustee name	1/16/2019	Yes	1	1	1	1			1	1			6
insert Civic Trustee name	insert Civic Trustee name	1/16/2019	Yes	1	1	1	1	1	1	1	1	1	1	7
insert Civic Trustee name	insert Civic Trustee name	1/16/2019	Yes	1	1	1		1		1	1			5
insert Civic Trustee name	insert Civic Trustee name	1/16/2019	Yes	1	1	1	1		1	1				5
insert Civic Trustee name	insert Civic Trustee name	1/16/2019	Yes	1			1			1	1		1	4
insert Civic Trustee name	insert Civic Trustee name	1/16/2019	Yes	1	1	1	1	1	1	1	1	1	1	8
insert Civic Trustee name	insert Civic Trustee name	1/16/2019	Yes	1			1	1	1			1		4
insert Civic Trustee name	insert Civic Trustee name	1/16/2019	Yes	1			1		1	1	1			4
insert Civic Trustee name	insert Civic Trustee name	1/16/2019	Yes	1	1	1	1	1	1	1	1	1		9
insert Civic Trustee name	insert Civic Trustee name	1/16/2019	Yes	1	1			1						3
insert Civic Trustee name	insert Civic Trustee name	1/16/2019	Yes	1	1	1								3
insert Civic Trustee name	insert Civic Trustee name	1/16/2019	Yes	1	1	1	1	1	1	1	1	1	1	8
insert Civic Trustee name	insert Civic Trustee name	1/16/2019	Yes	1	1	1	1		1	1	1	1	1	8
insert Civic Trustee name	insert Civic Trustee name	1/16/2019	Yes	1	1	1	1		1	1		1		6
insert Civic Trustee name	insert Civic Trustee name	1/16/2019	Yes	1	1	1	1	1	1	1			1	6
insert Civic Trustee name	insert Civic Trustee name	1/16/2019	Yes	1	1	1	1	1	1	1	1	1	1	8
insert Civic Trustee name	insert Civic Trustee name	1/16/2019	Yes	1	1	1	1	1	1	1			1	8
insert Civic Trustee name	insert Civic Trustee name	1/16/2019	Yes	1								1		2
insert Civic Trustee name	insert Civic Trustee name	1/16/2019	Yes	1	1	1	1	1	1	1	1	1	1	9
insert Civic Trustee name	insert Civic Trustee name	1/16/2019	Yes	1	1				1				1	3
insert Civic Trustee name	insert Civic Trustee name	1/16/2019	Yes	1	1	1			1	1			1	5

SAMPLE: RECAP MEMO

Hello City Civic Trustees,

Thank you for making last night another great meeting. We had a strong turnout with 3 new guests in attendance. Hopefully, we will see our guests attending next month as Civic Trustees.

To recap what was reported, The City School District has been making strides with getting social studies teachers prepared to teach Power Civics for High Schools, which is now permanently embedded in the high school social studies curriculum.

Thanks to your hard work and persistence, all US History II classes (a mandatory course needed for high school students to graduate) will be equipped to empower students to become No-Blame Problem Solvers in their city! The City Public Schools will also promote Civic Week to their high school students.

In addition, with the help of Civic Trustee Latoya W., Power Civics is being taught at the County College for the second semester. All of these successes combined are helping the City become recognized as a Civic City.

New Issue Committees were formed to address the following City challenges:

Current Issue Committees' progress includes:

That's it for now. Thanks again for your commitment to making our City better. If you get stuck on any of the work or assignments, don't hesitate to reach out.

Enjoy the rest of your week and I'll see all of you soon.

SAMPLE: CIVIC TRUST MEETING FLYER

SAMPLE: RESOLUTION OF SERVICE

RESOLUTION OF RECOGNITION FOR SERVICE AS A CIVIC TRUSTEE

Whereas, Civic Trustee_____(Name)_____ has taken the CIVIC PLEDGE to leave their City better than they found it, and has met the standards to qualify as a Civic Trustee; and

Whereas, said Trustee has completed training in the process of NO-BLAME PROBLEM SOLVING; and

Whereas, said Trustee has participated in monthly Solution Sessions for a minimum of one year for the purpose of finding, developing, and implementing government solutions to improve the City; and

Whereas, said Trustee has both by example and by outreach to others, promoted the values of unselfish service and mutual respect;

Now, therefore, be it resolved, that this Trustee be recognized and commended for their civic leadership as a CIVIC TRUSTEE of the City of _____.

_____
GOVERNOR JAMES FLORIO

_____
GOVERNOR TOM KEAN

_____
GOVERNOR CHRISTINE TODD WHITMAN

Dated:

SAMPLE: MODEL MEMO FOR POTENTIAL CIVIC TRUSTEE RECRUITS

Memo for Use by Recruiters

A Civic Trustee is a citizen who searches for and advances evidence based, cost effective Solutions for the benefit of their City. They use a proven No-Blame method and a practical approach to problem solving that was designed by a team of government policy experts, retired public officials and government law practitioners. Civic Trustees identify the issues they seek to resolve and search for successful policies to address their city's problems that are working in similar towns or cities.

Civic Trustees take responsibility for their community issues without ever pointing fingers or assigning blame. They engage their local public officials and administrators to join them in the search for proven solutions. Trustees' solutions have been adopted for use by their local governments, resulting in the adoption of over 300 laws with an over 90% passage rate. Civic Trustees are unselfish public servants who don't seek rewards or salaries. They have no political agenda; rather, they offer their skills, resources, and knowledge to find successful policies in cities similar to their own and import them for adoption in their own communities.

You can submit an application to become a Civic Trustee: Online through The Citizens Campaign website; on the Civic Trust Facebook page; or by completing a hard copy application (see Sample Application in this Handbook). If you were invited to a Civic Trust meeting, ask the Facilitator of the meeting for an application. Fill out the application and turn it in to the Facilitator or bring it with you to the next meeting.

On the application, make sure that you check the box stating you have taken the Civic Pledge. If you do not take the Civic Pledge, your application will not be approved. The Administrator will make arrangements for you to learn about the "No-Blame" approach, the commitments that Civic Trustees make, and the No-Blame problem solving process that Trustees use to find and implement solutions for their city.

Disqualifying Factors

Civic Trusts are non-partisan associations that focus on solving the issues affecting their hometowns. To ensure that all Trusts are run by regular citizens and that their work is not based on political or special interest agendas, citizens who are elected officials or their spokespersons, candidates, party chairs or party treasurers, or spokespersons, and campaign organizers cannot serve as Civic Trustees. If you have been a former elected official, party leader, or a campaign organizer, you can apply to become a Civic Trustee, as long as you commit to display non-partisanship and maintain the No-Blame discipline during your term as a Civic Trustee.

Should you participate in a partisan fashion, or assign blame publicly during your term, you will not be invited back to the Civic Trust and will no longer be considered a Civic Trustee. Public display of blame includes blame expressed in social media posts, blogs, conventional press, public presentations and forums. Each Civic Trustee is a representative of the Civic Trust. Expressing blame takes the focus off of solutions and undermines the credibility of your fellow Trustees. Contact the Help Desk if you have any questions regarding your public involvements.

Threshold Responsibilities of a Civic Trustee

There are three threshold responsibilities for serving as Civic Trustees.

1. Practicing the No-Blame Approach in all public venues;

2. Committing to attend monthly Civic Trust meetings for a period of one year (except during August and December);

3. Using the No-Blame Problem Solving method to find and advance solutions.

When all 3 responsibilities are taken seriously and practiced, Civic Trustees are able to keep the focus on the evidence based, cost-effective solutions they are advancing.

Taking the Civic Pledge

All Civic Trustees take this *Civic Pledge:*

"I pledge to leave my community and country better than I found them by pursuing practical solutions instead of just pointing out problems and assigning blame."

The *Civic Pledge* is based on a pledge taken by citizens of ancient Athens when they reached the age of maturity. It embodies a commitment to unselfish service to one's community and represents the core value of democracy. The *Civic Pledge* is a values proposition that is shared by and unites all Civic Trustees.

SAMPLE: CIVIC TRUST MEETING AGENDA

<u>City Civic Trust Agenda</u>

Our Next Meeting is:
Day, Month, Year   Day, Month, Year
Street Address   Street Address
City, State and Zip Code   City, State and Zip Code
                                          Please Mark Your Calendars

1) 5:30 PM to 6:00 PM   Dinner and fellowship with City Civic Trustees

2) 6:00 PM to 6:10 PM   Welcome Guests of the City Civic Trust

3) 6:10 PM to 6:20 PM   Introductions

4) 6:20 PM to 6:30 PM   Reports and Communications
                        from the Home Office

5) 6:30 PM to 6:50PM   Presentation: Guest Speaker and Q & A

6) 6:50 PM to 7:05 PM   New Issues: suggestions of Civic Trustees

7) 7:05 PM to 7:35 PM   Breakout Sessions: Issue Committees
                        assemble separately

8) 7:35 PM to 7:55 PM   Action Steps: Committees reconvene and
                        report on action steps

9) 8:00 PM   Clean up and adjourn.

SAMPLE: CIVIC TRUST MEETING PREP CALENDAR

	Mon	Tues	Wed	Thurs	Fri
Week 1			Draft an "update" of previous meeting and send to Trustees; include RSVP request for attendance at next meeting; Send Separate Invite to potential Trustees (add RSVP)		Send out invitation to Guest Speaker for next meeting; Post Civic Trust meeting on social media, add successes by the Trust; Send to local news media
Week 2	Fill in Agenda and send to Trustees for their input; Add a 2nd Request for RSVP				
Week 3	Email last request for RSVP	Call Committee members to get status of action steps			Last call or text to Trustees who did not RSVP; Confirm availability of facility, Facilitator and Guest Speaker
Week 4	Order food & confirm delivery; Finalize Agenda & make copies; Bring sign-in sheet, RSVP Roster, applications, "Get Results" form, misc. forms, handouts, articles, etc.	CIVIC TRUST MEETING; Supplies: bring pads and pens; Bring plates, utensils, servers, & water	Start over with Week 1		

SAMPLE: SIGN IN SHEET

The Civic Trust   **Sign In Sheet**   **Date**

If you are an active Civic Trustee and your contact information has not changed, you can sign in by filling out your name only. All others, please enter your full contact information.

Name	Phone	Email	How would you like to be reminded of the Trust meetings? (Email, Phone Call, Text, etc.)

SAMPLE: CIVIC TRUSTEE APPLICATION

Civic Trustee Application

Full Name

Phone   Email

Street Address   City   State   Zip

If you are currently employed, please list your employer and position:

What is your relationship with your City? (Check all that apply.)
- ❑ I LIVE HERE
- ❑ I WORK HERE
- ❑ I GO/WENT TO SCHOOL HERE
- ❑ I GREW UP HERE
- ❑ OTHER _____

Facebook Name: _____

Instagram Name: _____

Please indicate which issue areas you are most interested in:
- ❑ EDUCATION
- ❑ PUBLIC SAFETY
- ❑ ECONOMIC DEVELOPMENT
- ❑ GOVERNMENT EFFICIENCY & WASTE CUTTING
- ❑ ENVIRONMENT
- ❑ CITIZEN EMPOWERMENT
- ❑ OTHER

Continues on side 2

SAMPLE: CIVIC TRUSTEE APPLICATION

Please include a description of any community service or civic activity that you have been involved in and any examples of your taking a leadership position at work, in sports, in community or neighborhood activities, etc.

Will you serve as a Civic Trustee for one year? (This includes monthly meetings, except during August and December, with up to 3 excused absences permitted.)

Will you watch the 10 five minute Power Civics videos to prepare for becoming a Civic Trustee?

Do you have any additional information about yourself that you would like to share with us? *(You may want to share your current involvement in your community, what interested you to apply, or what you hope to gain as a Civic Trustee. Your response to this section is optional.)*

Taking the Pledge and joining your fellow citizens moves our communities and our country onto the powerful path of pragmatic problem solving. Will you take the Civic Pledge described below?

> ### THE CIVIC PLEDGE
> *I pledge to leave my community and country better than I found them by pursuing practical solutions instead of just pointing out problems and assigning blame.*

❑ Yes! Please count me among my fellow citizens who have taken the Civic Pledge.

SIGNATURE   DATE

SAMPLE: CIVIC TRUST MEETING FLYER

WANT TO LEARN HOW TO BECOME A CITY PROBLEM SOLVER?

BECOME A PHILADELPHIA CIVIC TRUSTEE

LEARN TECHNIQUES USED BY SUCCESSFUL PRACTITIONERS THAT TRANSFORM CITY ISSUES INTO SOLUTIONS!

NEXT MEETING

WEDNESDAY, APRIL 3, 2019 AT 6PM
COMMUNITY COLLEGE OF PHILADELPHIA
1700 SPRING GARDEN ST., PHILADELPHIA, PA

DINNER WILL BE SERVED, BUT YOU HAVE TO RESERVE!

FOR MORE INFORMATION
CALL CIVIC TRUSTEE
732-548-9798
OR EMAIL
THECIVICTRUST@GMAIL.COM

SAMPLE: MEDIA RELEASE

Applications Now Open for New City Civic Trustees
Join Together with Fellow Residents to
"Leave Your City Better than You Found It"

The City Civic Trust announced today that the application process for city residents wishing to become Civic Trustees is now open. The application period ends on February 15th. All applicants will receive free leadership training. Those who are accepted will enjoy serving with their fellow citizen leaders in a No-Blame environment with the support of top legal and policy experts, as they search for successful solutions to city problems.

The City Civic Trust is comprised of about 24 Civic Trustees who receive training in a proven method of No-Blame problem solving and come together in monthly solutions sessions. They work as problem-solving partners with elected and other city officials, putting forward policies that have worked in similar cities. They also serve as agents of empowerment, educating city residents about opportunities for civic leadership. Civic Trustees commit to serve for at least one year.

Applications will be reviewed on a first-come, first-serve basis. Visit www.thecitizenscampaign.org to submit an application or submit related questions.